A JOURNEY

TO BEGIN

McDougal & Associates
Servants of Christ and stewards of the mysteries of God

A JOURNEY

TO BEGIN

God, I Know You and You Know Me. What Else Is There to It?

by

Joanne Yoho

A JOURNEY TO BEGIN
Copyright © 2008—by Joanne E. Yoho
ALL RIGHTS RESERVED

Original cover design by Sherie Campbell
sonandshield@comcast.net

Published by:

McDougal & Associates
www.thepublishedword.com

McDougal & Associates is dedicated to the spreading of the Gospel of Jesus Christ to as many people as possible in the shortest time possible.

ISBN 13: 978-1-934769-09-6
ISBN 10: 1-934769-09-6

Printed in the United States of America
For Worldwide Distribution

Dedication

This book is dedicated to Abba Father, the God who loves me and whose mercies are new every morning, to His Son Jesus Christ, the one who has saved me from destruction and redeemed my life to the uttermost through His body and blood, and to the Holy Spirit, who has been my Teacher, Comforter and Helper without end.

ACKNOWLEDGMENTS

I want to thank God, our heavenly Father, for all the men and women who have gone on before me, whom He has used to pave the way for all to come to Him and to come to know Him. Also, for the many who have shared their faith in God the Father, God the Son, Jesus Christ, and God the Holy Spirit and in the Word of God, and for all their heartfelt testimonies. In particular, there are four men of old whom I cannot help but mention. They are Father Abraham, King David, Saint Peter and Saint Paul, and God used each of them to give me hope and change.

Why Father Abraham? Because he was the beginning, that is the first person of faith who believed and received what God said.

Why King David? Because he was the one considered least in a family of many sons, but he sang to God while tending his father's sheep. His songs are now called the Psalms, and they make up a great part of the book by that same name found in our Old Testament. I'm in those psalms all the time, and I value them greatly, as they reveal so much about God—that is, who He is, what He said and did—and the rest that I have yet to come to know. To me, the Psalms present something of a mini-highlight of all that can be found in the pages of the Bible.

Why Peter and Paul? Because here were two men so opposite in schooling and life status, and yet God wanted them—in spite of themselves. And what a journey they, too, began and had with God the Father, His Son Jesus and the Holy Spirit! Their course in life was dramatically changed by God to something far better and more wonderful than they would or could have dared hope for. The ways and truths God gave them and many others to pass on to us have encouraged and helped me immensely and are continuing to impact and cause good change and growth in me daily.

Why share all of this? Because, dear reader, this same God has a journey for you to begin! Will it be boring? No, not with God! Because He has a journey that will be just right for you! And with that having been said, let's start together *A Journey to Begin.*

THE JOURNEY

Everyone's on a journey,
knowing it or not,
coming to, coming out,
even coming through.

Life is a journey,
finding, gaining, losing,
going, staying, again coming,
new, then old, then more new.

A journey, a life given,
for one, to one, for all,
a really "neat" journey.

Come! Get up! Get unto yours!
It's a God-given one
meant to be, meant for all.

Even more, for Him,
yes, for Him to glory in!

—Joanne Yoho

CONTENTS

INTRODUCTION

Although my words may be simple, the thoughts expressed here come from my heart and soul, with God's inspiration. But please don't blame Him for any of my lacks. His Word teaches that He uses *"the foolish things of the world"*:

> *God hath chosen the foolish things of the world to confound the wise; and God hath chosen the weak things of the world to confound the things which are mighty; and base things of ... which are not, to bring to naught things that are: that no flesh should glory in his presence.* 1 Corinthians 1:27-29

It has always amazed me that God used me, and it continues to amaze me today. It is only by His grace.

My knowledge of God has begun, most often, with an experience. It was only later, through the help of the Holy Spirit, that my understanding of the experience caught up with my participation in the experience. Because of this, what I was experiencing was often totally new to me.

This may seem backwards to some. They first gain the knowledge or understanding of a thing, and then they experience it. All I can say is that it happened to me the other way around. I seemed to be coming at it from a totally different direction than most.

This didn't seem at all backwards to me. God's Spirit was dealing with my spirit. He would show me something, and sometime afterward I would hear the same thing preached or taught, or I would read it somewhere. I knew that what was being preached or taught or written was true because I had already experienced it—although I could not have explained it with chapter and verse at the time. I sensed God dealing with me long before I had much knowledge of Him. In time, the knowledge came, through spending time with Him and His Word.

Again, it has always been a wonder to me that God called me, for I wasn't what people were looking for. Often, I asked God why He wanted me when it seemed that no one else did. Why would He choose crumbs when He could have steak? One day, He answered me like this: "I know your potential." I never had to ask Him again.

Through the years, I often said to God, "You have put so much of Your Word into me and have otherwise invested so much in me that You should have a good return." Perhaps this book is part of that return. May it be a blessing to you, and may it enable you on your own personal journey with God.

A Journey to Begin is a little bit about my journey with God and a little bit about yours as well. How could it be about you? Well maybe you will sense it or hear it as you read along, perhaps in one of the chapters or even in all of them. So, if you have an easy chair, sit back and relax. You should find this to be an "easy read."

Joanne Yoho

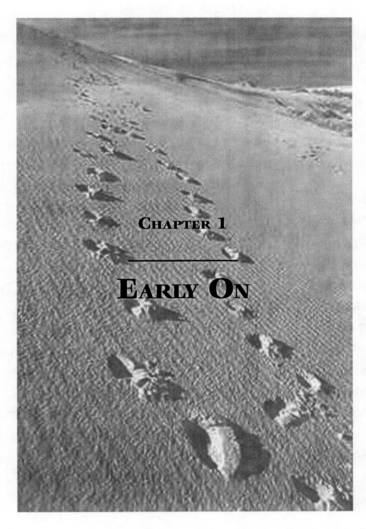

CHAPTER 1

EARLY ON

God is in the midst of her; she shall not be moved: God
shall help her, and that right early.   Psalm 46:5

I must begin my story as a young child playing under the porch of a three-story apartment building in the
city of Chicago, where my family lived during my early
years. As I recall, I was playing by myself under that

porch, when someone spoke to me and asked me a question. The question was: would I become a nun? My answer came without hesitation: no, for I wanted to be a mom like my own mother.

It never occurred to me that God Himself was speaking to me in that moment or that perhaps I was rejecting Him. It was simply a child's choice. Only much later did I give it more thought.

> *I was playing by myself under that porch, when someone spoke to me and asked me a question!*

That was the first choice I fully remember making that had anything to do with God (although I didn't know it at the time, and it's only in hindsight that I know it now). In reality, it was not just a choice I made; it was also an encounter with God that ever so quietly occurred. God was interested in the life of a young child.

How About You?

How about you? Do you recall any God encounters in your early years? Stop and think about it. What were your choices at the time? What did you think? What did you say? This is what I have come to call "a biggie," something so serious that you must consider it. Why? Because an encounter with the Almighty is something we must never take lightly.

At times, as we travel along life's journey, we get stopped. What has stopped us often seems to be an accident caused by life's demands, changes, challenges or distractions. But it also might be by choice, that is by you choosing to do just what you want to do at the moment. Not all of the choices we make in life produce what we have wanted or hoped for.

LACKING KNOW-HOW

For years, I felt very bad about lacking know-how in life. I seemed to have so many lacks. In reality, whatever lack I had was my own fault, for I hadn't applied myself sufficiently while I was still in school. Sure, I did the assignments. But did I study? No! I crammed enough to pass tests, but without really learning much in the process. I took books home with every good intention, but with my eyes and ears glued to the television screen at home ... Well, you know the rest. Being a bit slow and lazy didn't help either.

So education is something we all need, and we also need a certain wisdom that only comes from God. Without that important element, my journey would have been stalled a long time ago. I thank God that He was not only interested in me as a small child; He has continued to follow me throughout life.

SEEKING GOD'S WISDOM

Early in my journey, I was blessed in that I became

careful to seek for God's wisdom. That's very interesting, because I didn't know much about Him or His kind of wisdom. In the school system of our day, all we were taught was the need to gain knowledge. In the classroom, we were encouraged to memorize important dates and events, and then we were tested on what we had memorized, and we moved on to the next thing.

But something was clearly missing in all of this. What was it? It was much like the ingredients we put into a recipe to lend a meal flavoring. Foods require flavoring, even if it's not a lot. So what am I getting at? Life requires seasoning, spice, passion. And that only comes from God.

THE PASSION OF OUR FOREBEARS

Let me give you an example of what I mean by this. It wasn't until I flew over the Rocky Mountains and looked down at the rugged landscape that I understood what the men and women who crossed those mountains in covered wagons had accomplished. What courage! What strength! What suffering they must have endured! They often suffered the loss of all their belongings and, even more so, many of them lost their lives, and they did it to pave the way for our coming in the future. Just presenting the facts about these heroic feats performed by our forebears is not enough; we need to understand the passion and conviction that drove them to do what they did.

What so motivated these people that they put absolutely everything at risk? How could they do that? Was there not faith involved? There must have been. Were they not praying people? Surely they were, as most men and women still are today—when faced with a dead-end, an impasse or one of life's apparent tragedies.

SHOULD IT NOT BE PASSED ALONG?

Should not the passion and conviction that motivated men to make this such a great country be passed on? Is this not the very core and backbone of our country? In recent years, I've read books that declare this to be so. We Americans have lost so much, and one of our greatest losses is love of country and appreciation for those who went before us.

Another great thing was lost when God was systemically taken out of our educational system. In the process, love and honor for God were removed and no longer presented to our children. And that could only have produced disastrous results.

The faith in God that those who formed this country so nobly expressed is no longer evident in our children's textbooks. It seems that the men and women who volunteer to serve in our armed forces understand the greatness behind this nation. They're not forced to serve, and yet they enlist, knowing full well that they will be putting their lives in jeopardy. They do it because they believe in this nation and what it stands for.

IT'S TIME FOR THE TRUE HISTORY OF OUR NATION TO BE KNOWN

It's time that the true history of our nation and its people was returned to our classrooms. Most of the founding fathers of these United States of America were God-fearing and God-loving men who prayed in private and in public to be worthy of the office they held. Much of our constitution is based on God and the Bible. And when our education system was established, what God said in the Bible was taught all the way from the primary grades right up through the college level. Actually, the early colleges were begun by ministers to make sure there be others to follow them. College was a place to train men to become able ministers of the Gospel, and for other needed professions.

Therefore the conviction and passion that made this nation great must be passed on to the next generations. Instead, it is slowly being deleted from our history books. This is a mistake of monumental proportions.

SERIOUS CHANGES TO OUR EDUCATIONAL SYSTEM

Serious changes in our education system began in the middle 1800s and have continued ever since. Little by little, the foundations of our nation have been eroded. Doesn't it make you want to think? What has taken its place? What was the void filled with? This movement began with just a few leaders, and they didn't have as their motivation the separation of church and state. That concept, which is now at the forefront of the battle for our children's minds, only came into play many decades later.

What did the founding fathers really say about this matter? Their statements need to be read and understood in their context. They would not have dared to suggest that God be separated from our public schools, for there would have been too great a public outcry. Instead, a slow but steady erosion has taken place, and it was never the will of the majority.

Choices and decisions are being made all the time that affect our future as a people. We may be aware of some of them, but of most, we're not. But, although many wrong choices and decisions are being made concerning America, it's not too late to do something about it. Please pray for all those in leadership and/or authority instead of complaining about them, or worse yet, mocking and making sport of them. Your prayers can make a difference. Just talking about the problems often simply adds fuel to the fire and can even make matters worse.

Now, I know it seems like I got off track here, but not really, for our nation, too, had many God encounters, as well, in its early beginnings and along its way, and they are indeed recorded. I just wanted you to be aware of that, as well, as I continue on about personal encounters and choices with God.

When our education system was established, what God said in the Bible was taught all the way from the primary grades right up through the college level!

19

A JOURNEY TO BEGIN

MAKING THE RIGHT CHOICE

Some of you may know what I'm talking about when I speak of an encounter with God, but, for others, this may be the first time anyone has spoken to you in this way. Please don't be put off by such thoughts. Although I'm not an expert in anything, I have been on this journey with God for a good while now. As an experienced traveler, I would like to encourage anyone who has not yet begun this journey to do so now.

You have a choice in this matter. You can choose to come to know the God of all creation and then walk with Him. It's really a matter between you and Him. His name is Jesus, and He is the only Son of God, the one *"which was, and is, and is to come"* (Revelation 4:8).

APPRECIATING GOD'S NAMES

Jesus has many titles and names, as does our heavenly Father and the Holy Spirit (or Holy Ghost, as He is also called). God's various names are of total interest and even fascinating to me, as they each reveal who He is and what He does.

When you think about it, what's the first thing you get to know about a person when you meet them? It's their name, isn't it? Allow me to introduce you to one of the names for Jesus that really got my curiosity up. It is the name Door:

Then said Jesus unto them again, Verily, verily, I say unto you, I am the door of the sheep.　　John 10:7

Now, why would Jesus call Himself the Door? I didn't understand that until I heard someone explain what a good shepherd does for his sheep in the rocky caves around Bethlehem. When the sheep are safely in for the night, the shepherd positions himself in the opening of the cave in such a way that he becomes the door. Nothing can get past him and get to his sheep. So Jesus is our Door.

If you want a good starting place in your journey with God, look at His names, for they reveal so much about His character. While you're at it, talk to Him from your heart about His names and whatever else comes to mind. He will answer you.

BECOMING AWARE OF GOD

Early in life, I didn't have much to say to God, although I did during communion time at church. For sure, I talked to Him whenever I got myself into some real jam as a teenager, but that was the extent of my contact with God.

My growing-up years were problem free, as I remember them. When I came home from school, I did my required chores, and then I was free to go out and play. We had moved by then from Chicago to a small community, and especially in the summer time, there were no restrictions on me. I could swim as long as I wanted at the lake, spend time at a friend's house, play softball or other outside games (like tag, statues or red rover) until it got dark. Only then did my mom call me to come home.

A Thinking Child

> *I reasoned that if vocabulary was the measure of one's intelligence then mine would be seen as pretty low if I swore!*

I was a thinking child from early on, although others probably would not have guessed it. When situations arose, I was able to make decisions that would affect my future. For instance, although I told no one about it, I made the decision not to smoke the day I first tried it. I felt so dumb trying to get the hang of it. I thought to myself, I already feel dumb. Why feel this way on purpose? So I started smoking and stopped smoking on the same day.

I thought about what was required to lie effectively and decided against it. You would need a very good memory to get away with it, I decided, and I was not nearly that clever.

I thought about it and made the decision not to swear. Swear words were common, but I reasoned that if vocabulary was the measure of one's intelligence then mine would be seen as pretty low if I swore.

I made a conscious decision not to do anything to lose my mother's trust. I was blessed to have it, and I knew that if I lost it, I would no longer be allowed to go out freely. Therefore I tried to do what she said.

WHAT ABOUT YOU?

Before I go any further, let me share something with you that I'm realizing even as I write this. First, we think a thing. Then we make a decision. And that decision governs our actions from that moment on. I was making decisions that were to affect me for many years into the future, and I didn't even realize it at the time.

How about you? It's not too late to stop and think about your future and to make conscious decisions for good. I believe we all have these moments in our lives, but maybe we're just not aware of them. Chew on this for a while, if you would.

SHY WITH BOYS

I was very shy with boys and usually said no to their invitations to date. I was afraid I wouldn't know how to handle myself. I was very naive. It wasn't until I had met Bob after high school that I began to date seriously. I felt completely comfortable with Bob and trusted him early on.

When Bob first asked me to marry him, I told him no. I knew I wasn't in love with him, and thought to myself, "You can't fool with a guy, as he will eventually know that." When he pressed me for the reason, I declined to answer. He was a great guy, and I didn't want to hurt him. When he asked me for the third time, I decided not to hold back any longer. That was the end of our dating.

We would see each other at work. Actually, it was not hard to see him since his desk was right in front of mine. When he eventually asked me out again, I said yes, although I wasn't sure why, as I still wasn't in love with him.

I do remember the moment love for Bob came to my heart. It had to be from God. I was standing by the bedroom closet, getting dressed, when it suddenly dawned on me that I loved this man. It was another of those God moments.

The next time we went out, I told him. He was driving, and I said to him, "Bob, guess what?" And then I expressed my new-found love for him. He immediately pulled the car off the side of the road, both of us smiling and then decided to marry. I had a small calendar on my check register, and we used that to decide when our special day should be. Six months later we were married. I had turned twenty-one, and he was twenty-nine, but I never felt the age difference.

MARRIED LIFE LEADS TO SPIRITUAL LIFE

As life continued, God gave us four wonderful boys—one at a time. Along with a lot of cloth diapers to wash and 3 AM feedings to attend to, we had great times of cuddling and holding our children. We were busy for a while raising our little family, but as time went on, we got more and more involved in the church.

During one meeting, our priest spoke about an upcoming men's weekend. He called it a "Cursillo." Bob decided to go. It was to be all men, both married and single. That's about all I knew at the time.

When Bob came home, he didn't have a lot to say about his weekend, but he did encourage me to go the weekend that would be only for women, single and married, and he said some good things would happen. I later learned that the men had been instructed not to tell their wives any details about the Cursillo, just to be sure that we attended.

What Bob was saying, therefore, seemed rather vague, and I couldn't imagine being away from my family for a whole weekend. I would miss them all. Why should I go?

I knew that Bob could survive without me. He was a good cook in his own right and often cooked for the whole family, and although taking care of four boys was a handful, he assured me that he would get along just fine. In the end, I went, not because I wanted to, but because I sensed that Bob very much wanted me to. Why? I wasn't sure.

A WAKE-UP CALL

For me, the Cursillo (which, in Spanish, means "short course") was one of the ministries God used for people to have time apart with Him, where they were being revived, renewed or called into leadership. It was to become a wake-up call. Somehow I had been like Sleeping Beauty, totally unaware of what was happening around me, spiritually speaking. Although God is so very aware of us, we can sometimes be very little aware of Him. I did have some limited awareness of His existence, but aside from celebrating Christmas and Easter, I didn't know much more.

I had very little actual faith in Jesus. I believed that He was the Son of God, but beyond that, I knew very little about what He had said or done. Then I was invited to attend that Cursillo. Before I tell you what happened, I need to say something God would want you to hear.

GOD MOVES IN MANY WAYS

God has many fine ministries that He is in and works through, and they can be just for you. What matters and is important for you is to be in the place God has provided for you, to be where you can have time with God and speak heart-to-heart with Him, to be where you can hear and know what God has to say to you through the words His anointed people speak.

God gives us opportunity to get away for a weekend or a week, somewhere that you will not be interrupted (especially if you leave the phone off). So, when the invitation comes or something sparks your interest, do make plans to go to these meetings. Don't let reasoning or excuses get in the way. Plus, don't let money be the issue—even if it seems to be. Instead, ask God to make a way for you or help you know how you can manage to go. Any changes God brings about through your time away can and only will be for your good. It was for me when, in 1971, God used the Cursillo movement (that started years before in Spain). Plus, He used my husband's desire and gentle push to go, and that moved me along with God.

A JOURNEY WAS ABOUT TO BEGIN

After arriving at the site of the Cursillo, we were led to a room where beds were set up. I put my bag away, picked out a bed and then sat down on it, feeling like a fish out of water. I said to God, "Well, God, I know You, and You know me. What else is there to it?" I wasn't being a "smart aleck." That was just where I was spiritually at the moment, and I was speaking out of my heart to Him. Little did I know that a journey was about to begin.

The next morning, while giving his homily, the priest spoke of Saint Peter and how he was always putting his foot in his mouth. That got my attention because I could identify with Peter's tendency. This got me to thinking so

I put my bag away, picked out a bed and then sat down on it, feeling like a fish out of water!

deeply that I stopped listening and started talking to God inside myself, saying that I was sorry for how I was talking to my husband and turning him off, and that I was not trying to, and what would happen if I were doing so on purpose? You see, I sensed this was happening at home, but I didn't know what I was doing wrong, and the priest's words just brought it to mind. And so I couldn't help but talk to God about it right then and there.

These thoughts passed quickly, and a minute or so later I was back listening to the homily again. But then an odd thing happened. Tears began streaming down my cheeks. I wasn't really crying, and yet the tears kept coming. And they did not stop, and I didn't know what was happening to me nor why. The Mass had ended, but the tears kept coming. I asked an older lady sitting beside me if she knew what was going on with me, and all she said was, "It's all right, dear."

The Tears Stopped

Gradually the tears stopped, as I walked to the meal area, ate lunch and then went on to hear the afternoon speakers. Much of what they had to say seemed to go over my head, especially their talk abut piety (especially in relationship to Christian service), which was not in my vocabulary. How could I do service, I was thinking, when I have four children, and one of them is still a baby? I dismissed that thought as being totally impossible.

But the tears had affected me very deeply, and so, for days after I got home from the Cursillo, I kept asking

God, "What happened to me that day? I know something happened. What was it?"

After this had gone on for some days, one day I began to see something before me. I know now that it was a heavenly vision, but at the time I wasn't sure just what it was.

In my vision, I saw a bright and shining silver platter. As I looked at it, I realized that the platter was like my soul. It was now shiny and clean, for God had taken my soul in His hands and had cleansed it. In that moment, my question was answered, and I was fully satisfied. My tears had been the outward sign of what God was doing within, in the deepest part of my being.

THE WORD EXPLAINED IT

It was not until about five years later that I came across a scripture in the Bible that described what I had experienced. It was found in the New Testament in the little book of Titus, and I share it here for your benefit. It's a very important passage that should not be missed. It shows us what God has done for others (fortunately I am among them) and what He can do and wants to do for you as well:

> For we ourselves also were sometimes foolish, disobedient, deceived, serving divers lusts and pleasures, living in malice and envy, hateful, and hating one another. But after that the kindness and love of God our Saviour toward man appeared. Not by works of righteousness which we have done, but according to his mercy

he saved us, by the washing of regeneration, and renewing of the Holy Ghost; which he shed on us abundantly through Jesus Christ our Saviour; that being justified by his grace, we should be made heirs according to the hope of eternal life. Titus 3:3-7

This may be a lot for some to take in, but it's worth the effort. Let the truths contained in this passage simmer in your spirit for a while, like a pot of soup or stew, and then let God's Spirit help you begin to consume it. If you do, your life, too, will be changed.

WHAT TO SAY TO GOD?

This, then, was the moment in which I was born again. In that moment, I went from having a religion to having a real relationship with God. But I wouldn't want to give a wrong impression. My new life didn't come overnight. I had a lot to learn. I still do, but that's okay. Our God is unending, and we will be forever learning new truths about Him.

But, in the meantime, what should I do? What do you say to this God who knows everything? All I knew was

> *All I knew was the "Our Father" prayer, so that's what I said, but what was I to do next?*

the "Our Father" prayer, so that's what I said, but what was I to do next? Surely there was a lot more for me, but how was I to get it?

As I sat there and reasoned, the thought came to me, Just be honest and sincere and don't be a "phony-baloney." I know these are simple words, but they got me into the presence of the mighty King of kings, and I've been enjoying wonderful fellowship with Him ever since.

So, dear reader, this is what happened to me early on, and I encourage you to be real, honest and sincere with God and to say just what you feel with Him.

Yes, we must humble ourselves in His presence. It's always better to do it ourselves than to have to be humbled by Him. There is only one who should be High and Mighty, and that's God.

A CHANGE OF HEADSHIP

I must share something else that happened early on to this newborn in Christ. I was reading in the New Testament about Christ being the Bridegroom and that we are His Body or His Bride. As I thought about this, I saw the church I was in while growing up to be like my parents. When I married, I left them and joined my husband, so that we could start a new life together. I didn't dismiss my parents, and I wasn't about to dismiss my church. What was about to change was the headship. After I was born again (in my late twenties), I became joined to Jesus Christ, and a new life in the Spirit began for me.

Christ Jesus is the very Head of His Body, the Church,

and He was meant to be so. My life was now under that new leadership, and Jesus Christ was my Head, not any denomination. When I went to church, it was to worship our Lord *"in spirit and in truth."* Jesus Himself said:

> *But the hour cometh, and now is, when the true wor-shippers shall worship the Father in spirit and in truth: for the Father seeketh such to worship him. God is a Spirit: and they that worship him must worship him in spirit and in truth.* John 4:23-24

Is my worship perfect in this sense? Probably not, but I ask the Lord to help me learn and do what His Word said to me. I was on a totally new course.

GOD IS OUR KING

This new life with and in Christ Jesus is a life of com-ing to know and knowing and hearing God, plus being helped and directed by God, His Son, His Word and His Holy Spirit. So what I left was religion, and what I now entered into was relationship—even communion and fel-lowship with God's Son, Jesus. And He offers that same thing to everyone. He does not wish that any should per-ish, but that all should have eternal life with Him. Again, Jesus Himself said it:

> *For God so loved the world, that he gave his only be-gotten Son, that whosoever believeth in him should not perish, but have everlasting life.* John 3:16

Just to whet your appetite some more, in the future there will be what is called in scripture *"the marriage supper of the Lamb"* (Revelation 19:9). Believe me, you surely don't want to miss that!

I'M THANKFUL FOR THE CHURCH

I'm thankful for the church I was able to attend until my late thirties, for it was a place of hearing about God, and you can be thankful about your church as well. I'm also thankful for the very large church I went to as a young child, before we moved from the city. It had great beauty, and there was always a holy reverence and a holy quietness there.

It was a place to kneel before God, and this was required off and on during the service. Kneeling and/or bowing down before the Lord is such a good practice to adopt. When you feel that you should do this, please don't hesitate—even when it's uncomfortable. Kneeling and bowing before God is honoring to such a mighty, great and faithful Father and to our Lord and Savior, Jesus Christ, the King of Glory.

HUNGRY FOR MORE OF GOD

After I was born again, I was very hungry for God and for His truth. Before then, this had not been the case. Now, some of the words said in the Mass came alive for me. When I heard the priest declare: "Christ has died, Christ has risen, Christ will come again," my heart leapt, and, for the first time, I knew that it was true. Jesus really was coming back again!

Until that moment, I had never thought about this future event, even though I had heard this phrase repeated over and over through the years. I was steadily growing in God and in faith, without really knowing it, something like a newborn does in its first year. Newborns are unaware of the growth that's going on with them, but it's phenomenal, and others notice it.

It wasn't until much later in my life that a big change of church attendance occurred, without my asking for it. It came about one Sunday morning, when my husband Bob asked me, "How was church?" We had gone to separate church services so that one of us could stay home with the baby. We were both home now, and I was standing in the kitchen making scrambled eggs for the whole family. I didn't seem to have a ready answer for him on that or several other questions he was asking me. Then a funny thing happened.

A Funny Thing Happened

After Bob had asked the question and waited for a moment for my answer, he answered it himself. I don't recall exactly how the question was worded, but when he answered, I remember turning around from the stovetop and saying to him, "Yes, it was all that!"

To my surprise, Bob replied, "Well, you can go to that church if you want to. Just take the babies with you." "The babies" were a six month old and a toddler, and, known only to God at the time, our last child, born one year later. The "church" he was referring to was one I attended on Wednesday evenings for Bible study. It never occurred to me to change churches or denominations, and I wasn't dissatisfied with my church. I simply wanted more of God.

I later wondered to myself how I could have changed so easily, and the way I came to understand it was this: there was a steady progression going on in my life, and going to church was much like going to school, where one passes from grade to grade. That's what was happening with me. I was moving along, coming to know more about God.

When I would run into a friend at the grocery store, and they would ask where I was attending, I would openly tell them where the Lord had led me to go. Some of them thought that I had left God. "To the contrary," I would tell them. "I have more of God now than ever." By their face, I could tell they weren't sure this could be true, but I knew it was.

Until that moment, I had never thought about this future event, even though I had heard this phrase repeated over and over through the years!

RELIGION VS. RELATIONSHIP

There's a distinct difference between religion and relationship. Religion is made up of a lot of tradition based partly on God's truth and partly on things men have made up. Religion contains a lot of dos and don'ts. Relationship, on the other hand, is not based on law, but on love. Respect, honor and an inner conviction by God's Spirit and His Word causes us to stop wrongful actions and begin to go God's way. He works with our hearts, not just our minds. And that's a big difference!

It was only by the grace of God and through His Son Jesus, His Spirit and the truth found in His Word that I began to change. And I do mean change! I was transformed from the inside out, and I know that I could never have achieved that on my own.

God used Bob at several pivotal moments of my life. In later years, I asked him one day why it was that he would let me go to other churches to learn about God. His answer was very wise: "I'm not getting in the way of God!" Thank God for that.

So, dear reader, this was some of my beginnings, what happened to me early on, long before I started taking any meaningful steps.   ❦

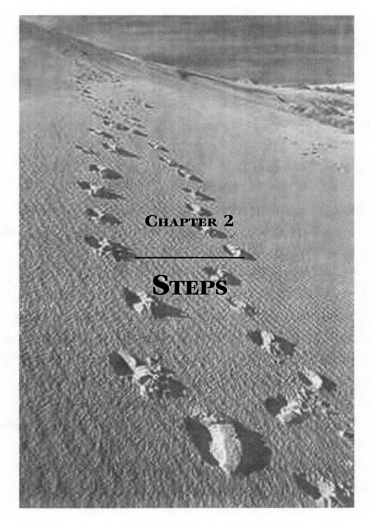

CHAPTER 2

STEPS

The steps of a good man are ordered by the LORD.
Psalm 37:23

Steps? Yes, baby steps. This born-again experience parallels the life of a newborn.

Is It Necessary?

Is it necessary to be born again? Oh, yes. According to the Bible, this is the only way to get into God's Kingdom. That's why Jesus said:

Ye must be born again.   John 3:7

Once a certain person approached me where I was sitting, stood there for a moment, and then suddenly asked, "Is it true that you must be born again?"

I looked up at this person and said, "Yes."

They clearly didn't like my answer, for they walked away in a huff. I'm not sure what made this person curious, because I hadn't been talking about this new birth with anyone. I barely understood it myself at the time. I had never once heard the phrase *"ye must be born again"* while I was growing up—even in church. But God said it, and it happened to me. I could not deny it. It was, indeed, truth.

I have come to learn that two things are very important to us in this journey called life. (1) What does God have to say about a given thing in His Word, the Bible? and (2) What did Jesus say and do about it when He was here on earth? He set the pattern for us to follow.

For instance, was Jesus baptized as a baby? No! Mary and Joseph took Him to the Temple, and there they dedicated Him to God. The Bible doesn't say much of His childhood, except for the fact that *"Jesus increased in wisdom and stature, and in favour with God and man"* (Luke

2:52). By the age of twelve, He was teaching others in the synagogue and doing it with great authority.

JESUS' BAPTISM

The actual baptism of Jesus came much later, when He was already an adult, and it was performed by His cousin, John the Baptist. In the process, Jesus was fully immersed in water, and when He came out of the water, He was filled with the Holy Ghost and power. Why did the Son of God need the Holy Ghost and power? For the ministry that had been entrusted to Him.

And what was Jesus' ministry? What did He go about doing? Well, for starters, He healed the sick, cast out demons and delivered all who were oppressed of the devil. He did a lot of teaching. Sometimes it was one on one, and sometimes it was to thousands at a time.

Now, could a baby do all that? No! Jesus first needed time to grow, not only in body, but in the knowledge and wisdom of God.

What does God have to say about a given thing in His Word, the Bible? and What did Jesus say and do about it when He was here on earth?

Now, I know this is the briefest of summaries, so it would pay you to read what we call the gospels, the books of Matthew, Mark, Luke and John. In them, you will find much more detail about Jesus' life and teachings, and you won't be sorry you took the time to read them.

MY CO-WORKER WAS ENTHUSIASTIC FOR HER FAITH

In my early twenties, I had a co-worker who would speak of her faith with great enthusiasm. That interested me. My faith was tepid as best. I couldn't give her a coherent answer as to why I put ashes on my forehead at lent.

This was a great beginning lesson for me, for her devotion caused me to reflect on the fact that I didn't really know much about my own faith. In hindsight, the big difference between the two of us was that she studied the Bible, by herself and with others, while I only heard it read on Sunday mornings at church.

I WAS HUNGRY

Some years later, when I began attending a Bible study at a Baptist church, the priest at my own church found out about it and wasn't very happy.

I hadn't tried to hide the fact that I was going to Bible studies at another church. I was hungry to know God and to know His truths, but the priest didn't understand this.

One afternoon he confronted me in the church parking lot about it. Why was I going to another church? he demanded, and in the process, threatened to take back a cross he had given me.

I was very timid and not a very vocal person, but that day I looked right at him and said, "If you had a Bible study here, I wouldn't have to go elsewhere." He knew it was true, so there was nothing more he could say. He turned and walked away.

It was a very awkward moment. I liked that priest a lot, and I had gotten a lot from the Bible studies he taught. But, for some reason, they had stopped and had not resumed. I was a very hungry newborn, and the need to seek God, His ways and His truth was a powerful force within me. I didn't cry about what wasn't available; I just went looking till I found what I needed.

Dear reader, these may be new words and thoughts for you, but know that it is important and that being born again is a very real event for all to come to, as is being baptized.

BEING BAPTIZED

Speaking of being baptized, I didn't really understand the need to be baptized after being born again. Some friends told me I needed it, and they asked me to go with them to a baptismal service being conducted in someone's pool. At first, I didn't feel good about it. After all, I had been baptized as a baby. But, as time went on, I sensed that I should do it.

All I could think was that Jesus had come into my heart when I was born again, but that I was fully into Him only after baptism!

Still I had some doubts, so I started seeking God about whether or not I should go. I didn't want to do something I shouldn't do. The Lord used His Word to give me an inner assurance that going would be the right thing to do.

I went to the baptism in faith, believing God and His Word, and as I was put down into the waters by a man of God and baptized in the name of the Father, the Son and the Holy Ghost, I held my nose. Moments later, I came up, and I proceeded to walk around the pool to a place where I could change back into some dry clothes. But as I walked, something began to happen within me.

Suddenly, I had a great joy on the inside. It made me think of the joy I'd felt the day Bob and I were married, plus thinking, "There's more to being baptized than we sometimes recognize." Years later, when I would hear a pastor say that baptism was only "symbolic," I would think to myself: Maybe, but it must be far more than that to God. Surely I could not have manufactured such tremendous joy!

What Happened to Me?

I wondered about that. What had happened to me? All I could think was that Jesus had come into my heart when I was born again, but that I was fully into Him only after baptism. I then found confirmation in the words of Jesus:

Jesus answered and said unto him [Nicodemus, a ruler of the Jews], Verily, verily, I say unto thee, Except a man be born again, he cannot see the kingdom of God. Nicodemus saith unto him, How can a man be born when he is old? can he enter the second time into his mother's womb, and be born?
Jesus answered, Verily, verily, I say unto thee, except a man be born of water and of the Spirit, he cannot enter into the kingdom of God. That which is born of the flesh is flesh; and that which is born of the Spirit is spirit. Marvel not that I said unto thee, ye must be born again. The wind bloweth where it listeth, and thou hearest the sound thereof, but canst not tell whence it cometh, and whither it goeth: so is every one that is born of the Spirit.   John 3:3-8

No One Needs to Be Left Out

No one needs to be left out of God's Kingdom, but it is clear that those who refuse to believe on Jesus Christ, (whom God sent to be our Savior), and receive Him as such surely will not enter in. I'm not trying to disturb people by these words, but this is something we all need to know and consider.

We must also know that there was a wonderful (and terrible) price paid for our admittance into God's Kingdom. This was when Jesus allowed His body to be beaten, pierced and torn, thus shedding His blood for us and for the sins of the whole world.

Jesus had no sin of His own, so what He suffered was entirely for us. As God in the flesh, Jesus was a truly perfect man, and He became a perfect sacrifice for us, all because God, our heavenly Father, loved us so much. As we have noted in the previous chapter, His desire is that none should perish but that all should have eternal life (see John 3:16).

By now, you might be wondering why you bought this book. You may have heard all of this before. But if God is so great, you reason, then why does He allow bad things to happen? Why doesn't He do something to prevent wars, famines and pestilence? You may have prayed, and there was no answer. At least not what you had hoped for, wanted or expected. Would a God of love fail to answer you in this way?

WHY DOES GOD GET ALL THE BLAME?

Let me address this important issue. Have you ever noticed that little or nothing is said these days of the one who comes *"to steal, kill and destroy"* (John 10:10)? Who am I talking about? The devil, or Satan. He is the enemy of God and also of you. He is not only a thief; he is also the *"father"* of lies:

Ye are of your father the devil, and the lusts of your father ye will do. He was a murderer from the beginning, and abode not in the truth, because there is no truth in him. When he speaketh a lie, he speaketh of his own: for he is a liar, and the father of it. John 8:44

Satan is the author of all evil, but when do you ever hear about that? Instead, God gets all the blame for the bad things that happen and very little acknowledgment for all the good He does. Men are so slow to give Him praise.

THE BATTLE FOR THE SOUL OF MAN

Please know this: there is a battle going on for the souls of men, and it has raged since God created the first man and woman—Adam and Eve. We've all been stolen from, lied to and deceived, and many have already been killed, and all this is going on with most having little or no knowledge and understanding that it's all Satan's work.

On the other hand, there is Someone who is far greater than man. He is not only the Creator of Heaven and Earth; He is the Almighty, the Most High God. He is even now creating a New Heaven and a New Earth. I've barely seen this first earth, and yet we will have a whole new earth to explore. And, as for Heaven, both the old and the new have to be great!

THE EXISTENCE OF ANGELS, FALLEN AND OTHERWISE

Aside from God, there are other heavenly creatures

45

known as angels. There are so many of them that they hold ranks and have leaders among them.

Angels are not people. They help people in one way or another and usually are not seen. Of these original angels, about a third failed to keep their place, rebelled against God and were cast down. Their leader was one called Lucifer. He is now known as Satan, the devil or even the dragon. That explains his power, doesn't it?

Obviously the fallen angels are not a happy group. How could they be? Their future has been sealed, and a place of punishment has been reserved for them. It is the opposite of Heaven and is known as Hell. Eventually they will all be cast into what is known as the Lake of Fire. The point is: Hell is not just a swear word, but a very real place intended for those rebellious angels and those who follow them.

WHO'S TO BLAME?

Now, getting back to the subject of who's really to blame when bad things happen: since it cannot be God, then who is it? It's the devil first, but it's also the result of our own sin, our own bad choices in life. Both of these entered into what was once a perfect world, the one through deception and the other through disobedience. Because of God's great love, He has a plan for each of us and has designated steps we need to take to come to Him and be cleansed of our sin. Many choose, instead, to take steps that lead them away from Him.

Taking steps toward God or away from Him is a choice,

a decision each of us must make, and it's yours alone to make. God will never force you to love Him, to believe Him or to accept Him.

We cannot say the same for the devil. His ways are deception and half-truths, along with a whole lot of temptation, and all of this is designed to get us to fall away from the Creator and be ensnared with what seems, for the moment, to be genuine "fun." It tastes good, and it dulls our pain or fills some void within us. But Satan's sure intent is to pull us into darkness, where we will be held captive and made to do as he wishes. Usually all of this occurs without us knowing it, except that occasionally God's Holy Spirit nudges our conscience in an attempt to get our attention. Whether we respond or not is up to each of us individually.

THERE IS HOPE

I know this may be hard to hear or may be hard to take in, but do give ear to what God has to say in the New Testament:

Because of God's great love, He has a plan for each of us and has designated steps we need to take to come to Him and be cleansed of our sin!

47

*And that they may recover themselves out of the snare
of the devil, who are taken captive by him at his will.*

2 Timothy 2:26

A *"snare"* is an unseen trap set for an unsuspecting prey, and in this case, we are the prey. This may make our situation seem rather hopeless, but look with me at what Jesus said to Saul of Tarsus, later Saint Paul:

*To open their eyes, and to turn them from darkness to
light, and from the power of Satan unto God, that they
may receive forgiveness of sins, and inheritance among
them which are sanctified by faith that is in me [Je-
sus].*

Acts 26:18

Yes, God can open your eyes, turn you from darkness to light and (the "biggie") from the power of Satan unto God. Why will He do that? So that you may receive forgiveness of sins, plus and inheritance among them that are sanctified by faith that is in Him. I know I just restated the whole verse, but the most important thing is this: He, Jesus, can do it. The question **is** will you let Him?

Sin Is Addictive

Please don't allow your love for some sin to rob you of getting out of darkness and out from under the power of Satan. Some sins are so addictive that it takes Jesus to deliver you from them. But He can do that. Again, will you let Him?

Remember, you can talk this all over with Him. Please take the time you may need to do so. He is there for you, with great love and mercy. Your deliverance may come suddenly, or it may be a process, because an entire life-style is being addressed. So, whatever the case, let it begin.

THE UNSEEN BATTLE

So, yes, indeed, there is a battle going on, it's pretty much unseen, and it's in a place called "the heavenlies" (not Heaven itself). That battle is real and very intense, and it's all about you.

Though many don't like to consider it, there's a Heaven to gain and a Hell to shun. So, dear reader, there is a choice and a decision to be made by you, a step to be taken, and I urge you to take it now.

Being born again was a great first step for me, for with it, my journey to and with God began—even though I didn't know anything—just like a newborn doesn't know anything. In God, you will be greatly loved, nurtured and taken care of all your life, even when you don't believe or think so, because God is a Father to us—no matter what our age.

I CHOSE TO BELIEVE

Let me tell you about a choice I made one night while driving home over a country road. It was about 10 PM, and all around me was nothing but open space. Ahead I could

"Well, God, I don't know if You are or You're not, but I choose to believe that You are— based on those beautiful stars against that black sky!"

see only a vast black sky filled with stars. It was so stunning that I thought to myself, There must be a God! Look at all those stars! And they're not falling from the sky!

I know this may sound simplistic, and it's easily explained scientifically, but the thought of it got me to make a decision right then and there and to say a prayer. The prayer was this: "Well, God, I don't know if You are or You're not, but I choose to believe that You are— based on those beautiful stars against that black sky." I drove on for five miles or so without giving this any more thought.

Looking back on this experience later, it surprised me to think that way, as I had been attending church my whole life, but still I hadn't realized what a God moment that was or that I'd needed to settle something. Without me knowing it, there was a gap in my faith, and it was a big one—belief in God's very existence.

How about you? Do you have some gaps in your faith, in what

you believe? If so, then talk it over with God, or better yet, let God fill in the gaps. He's able to do that.

SEVEN YEARS LATER

Well, dear reader, I don't want to leave you hanging. There was an answer to that heartfelt prayer, but it came only after seven years. I'm not sure why it took so long, although I've heard that God doesn't count time like we do. To Him, a thousand years are as one day, and a day is as a thousand years (see 2 Peter 3:8). Maybe I just needed to be in faith for a while, that is, having faith for what was hoped for, even when the evidence was not yet seen.

Anyhow, one day, while I was standing in my living room, seven years later, suddenly (and I do mean suddenly), there was like a clap inside of me, and at once I knew. I immediately said out loud, "You are! You really are!" Then I thought, What I accepted on faith has suddenly become very real and sure to me.

What happened? Did I see someone? No. Did I hear someone? No. So what really happened? Well, there was a major witness in my spirit, so strong that I felt it. And right then and there I went from faith to absolute belief that God really existed.

I'M STILL LEARNING

Those were a few of my baby steps. Of course, I'm still learning to walk with God, His Son Jesus and His Holy Spirit. So, dear reader, be encouraged and give God your faith to work with and through. If you have put your faith "on the shelf," so to speak, or have discarded it for any reason, go get it, dust it off and start using it again. Maybe someday you'll be telling me your story, and I'll be glad to hear it. ❧

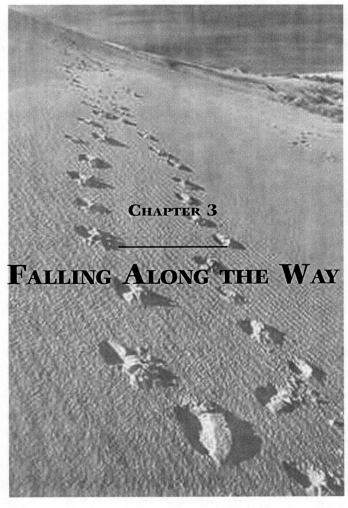

CHAPTER 3

FALLING ALONG THE WAY

*And let us not be weary in well doing: for in due sea-
son we shall reap, if we faint not.* Galatians 6:9

In a way, I have told you the beginning and the end, or, better said, given you some highlights of them, in these first two chapters. But there's also a middle—a big middle—and it is in the journey itself. It includes a lot of walking in the Spirit, praying in the Spirit, being led by the Spirit, and this "Spirit" is none other than the very Spirit of God. So this middle part is very exciting, especially when God moves in your life!

EVER LEARNING

In this journey with God, I was ever learning about my new life with Christ and His Spirit, but at times I would come to a place of not knowing just how to proceed or what exactly to think on next. That was okay with me, because it just caused me to say to God, "Now what?" Sometimes I actually had to say, "God, I've lost the way (or gotten off track), and I need Your help!"

So don't be surprise or bothered when you fall, as you move along on your journey with Christ and His wonderful Holy Spirit. It does happen, as there are lots of things that can cause us to trip and fall down. The important thing is to get up. If you stayed down, that *would* be a tragedy, and the consequences could be eternal.

What do I mean by this? Let me explain a little.

At times I would come to a place of not knowing just how to proceed or what exactly to think on next!

WE WERE MEANT TO TRIUMPH

God speaks to us in His Word, the Bible, about over-coming and triumphing. We were meant to overcome any obstacle that gets in our way as we journey. How? By being sober and vigilant. Why is that? For, as we have noted, there is one, who, like a roaring lion, goes about seeking whom he can devour. Peter urged us to resist him by standing firm in our faith (see 1 Peter 5:8-9). We can also overcome him by the blood of the Lamb and the word of our testimony (see Revelation 12:11).

A powerful weapon that I have often used against Satan is to testify through prayer. I pray things like this: "Thank you, Abba Father, for always causing me to triumph in Christ Jesus!" These are His words (see 2 Corinthians 2:14), and when I focus on His words, it's very powerful. I pray and declare this out loud whenever the Holy Spirit brings it to my mind.

Let me say this again. The beginning is important and the end is important, but there is a big middle that is also important. It includes living and moving along on your journey step by step. It means living a new life with Christ and with His Spirit.

LOOKING FOR FRUIT

We cannot see Him, and yet we can know Him and know that He is with us. How? One way is by what the Bible calls *"the fruit of the Spirit."*

Let me explain this a little. There are fruits from everything in life, and they are visible. There are, in fact, two different kinds of fruit that we can produce. The first kind of fruit comes forth from the flesh, and the second one comes from the Spirit. Here's how the apostle Paul described it to the Galatian believers:

> *Now the works of the flesh are manifest, which are these; Adultery, fornication, uncleanness, lasciviousness [lust], idolatry, witchcraft, hatred, variance, emulations, wrath, strife, seditions, heresies, envyings, murders, drunkenness, revellings, and such like. ...*
> *But the fruit of the Spirit is love, joy, peace, longsuffering, gentleness, goodness, faith, meekness, temperance.*
> Galatians 5:19-23

So, why tell you all this? Because the fruit of the flesh can cause you to fall, or, at the very least, it can trip you and make you nearly fall. So we must do all that we can to rid ourselves of it.

Think of these fruits as nasty potholes that can keep you from going forward. The sooner they are repaired the better it is for everyone.

The Spirit of Christ in you will enable you to decrease the fleshly fruit and enable you to have a better fruit, one that comes from the Spirit. To develop such fruit is not an overnight process. It takes time.

It's so wonderful to experience this better fruit, although plowing under (so to speak) the flesh to make it happen is not always a pleasant experience. This is necessary, however, if the new Spirit fruit is to come forth in us.

Sometimes it was a struggle for me to let go of my self, my flesh. Asking God to help me was my only answer. Sometimes I would say, "Help me, God! I'm stuck with myself!" In those moments, God could easily have condemned me (and with great cause), but He never condemns those who are in Christ Jesus (see Romans 8:1).

GOD HAS PUT HIS FAITH IN US

So there is a life with Christ and His Holy Spirit, whom I can come to know personally, even as I can know what He spoke for our benefit thousands of years ago. But guess what? God has left it up to us to believe and to receive. Oh my, what faith our heavenly Father has put in us!

I'll bet you never thought about it like that before. I hadn't until this very moment. Isn't it amazing how much God trusts us! When was the last time you created something and then willingly and freely gave it to your children and said, "Take care of this for me"? If God has entrusted so much to us, surely we should respond to Him.

FAITH FOR AND FAITH AGAINST

Everything takes faith, but there seem to be two kinds of faith: one is for and the other is against. You are either believing, or you are not believing. The in-between point would be moving toward faith or moving away from faith (and toward unbelief).

Sometimes it takes time for me to ponder over the Scriptures again and again until a moment when the Spirit of God moves on me, and then, by the grace of God, the truth of it clicks in my spirit. So, at times, you too may need to give yourself and God the time needed for you to believe and receive. And in that process, your faith increases.

Sure, God can and does reveal His truth to us very quickly, but there are times when my internal "junk" gets in the way. For example, a frozen mindset, a stronghold of some kind or even me just being stubborn or unyielding. I always ask God to help me rightly divide His Word of truth, and He does. And why does He do this? He wants us to know Him in the right way.

Please know that there is a pull and tug going on for your faith (or what you believe), and it involves not only your relationship with God, but also every aspect of your life. Each of us has been given a *"measure of faith"* (Romans 12:3), and this measure of faith is meant to increase, to grow.

Really, when you stop to think about it, all of creation is alive and growing. Even the universe is said to be expanding, and it would seem that it's already pretty big. Your faith was meant to grow too.

OUR OWN WORST ENEMY

Sometimes we are our own worst enemy and are unwittingly working against ourselves and, without knowing it, causing our fall along life's way. Could this be because so little good was said for us or about us early in life? Perhaps others didn't believe in us or for us, so we were left with little faith in ourselves or in who we are or what we can accomplish in life. Or maybe we were just left to try to figure life out on our own. Whatever the case, a struggle begins in us as we try to become the person we were destined to be and perhaps were even moving toward being—before someone squashed us or put us down in some way.

Sometimes our problem is that our own choices have not been the best, and they set us on a path contrary to the direction we were meant to walk in. Sometimes we simply wanted what we wanted, without realizing the cost, the very negative cost, to our future.

But one thing is so wonderful and so sure: God didn't forget what He had in mind for and with you and your precious life, and after you come into His Kingdom, while in this, His good earth, you will find God, who is love, is all about forgiving, healing, delivering and yes, restoring you.

Sure, God can and does reveal His truth to us very quickly, but there are times when my internal "junk" gets in the way!

A JOURNEY TO BEGIN

SOMEONE TO GET YOU UP WHEN YOU FALL

There are many reasons we fall along the way, but know this: there is One who wants to help you to get up and start moving again. It is, of course, God, our heavenly Father. He sent His only begotten Son, Jesus, the Christ, into this world specifically to help us. And, He, in turn, while on the cross, spoke and said, *"It is finished"* and then He *"gave up the ghost"* (John 19:30). He is now seated at the right hand of His Father (and ours), interceding for us day and night (see Romans 8:34).

You would think that with all Jesus did ... His teachings, His healings, His delivering of those who were in bondage to evil spirits, plus all the miracles that are not even recorded, it would be enough. But then, His body was beaten to a pulp, so that He no longer looked human (see Isaiah 52:14), and His blood was shed for you and me and all of mankind—even those not yet born. At this point, again, you would think that it would be enough. But no! He continues to intercede day and night for us all. How wonderful this is, indeed!

Surely our Lord Jesus Christ is wonderful and a wonder to me! For one thing, it's wonderful how He saves. He saved me, and I wasn't even looking for Him. As a matter of fact, I didn't know anything about being saved.

Saved from what? Saved from eternal punishment, never-ending punishment, and also from being banished from the presence of God forever and being sent to a very real place of torment, where there is *"weeping and gnashing of teeth"* (Matthew 24:51 and 25:30).

PLEASE DON'T CONSIDER TAKING YOUR OWN LIFE

As a side note, if you are contemplating taking your own life (for all of the very real reasons that have been in your thoughts), please know that there is a spiritual struggle going on for your body, soul and spirit. So please consider this: you and your future must have a value far greater than you can know right now or even believe. Otherwise, such great trials and temptations would not have come your way. Please believe this, and realize that your thoughts of taking your own life must not be acted upon.

How can I say that? Because, if you think that taking your own life will mean that your troubles, or trials, will be over and done for, I've got news for you, and it's all bad news at that. Rather than your problems being over, a whole new set of problems will be just beginning, and they will be like nothing you have ever thought about or bargained for. What's worse, once you're in that awful place, there can be no getting out or away from the torment—ever. And that is the awful and absolute truth.

DON'T SUFFER IN SILENCE

Please don't suffer in silence. I know what I speak, for I have been doing so for years. And God, by His Holy Spirit, revealed to me, and now to you, not to suffer in silence. Instead we should cast our cares upon Him.

And why should you cast your cares upon Him? Because, the Scriptures tell us, He cares for you (see 1 Peter

> *Christ's blood was shed for the sins of all mankind, and that same blood purges our conscious from dead works ... so that we can serve the living God!*

5:7). Ask Jesus to help you. Simply say, "God, help me not to do this thing! Help me to choose life!"

Run to the only One who can give rest to your soul. Performing a self-execution will never bring you the hoped-for end. It will only bring increasing and nonstop torment. Do you really want that, when Jesus offers you rest?

I know that Hell is not a pleasant topic to discuss, but you should know what your eternal home will be like. Will you live in what the Bible calls *"the lake of fire ... , the second death"* (Revelation 20:14-15)? It would pay to check out what the New Testament has to say about this place and about the alternative, Heaven. Read it for yourself. Never ever make a death choice. Hear?

JESUS TOOK OUR PLACE

More than two thousand years ago now, Jesus took my place (and yours) on the cross. We should have died there. Some didn't believe on Him then, and some don't believe on Him now, but believe me when I tell you that He is very much alive, and one day He will come back to this earth to receive His own. Believe me, on that day, you will really want to be His.

When He comes, first, those who have died in Christ will arise (see 1 Thessalonians 4:16), and then those who are still alive will be *"caught up ... to meet the Lord in the air"* (1 Thessalonians 4:17). This will be a great day for those who have believed and a very hard, terrible and grievous day for those who have not and those who would not. Believe today that He is the Messiah, the very Son of God. His blood was shed for the sins of all mankind, and that same blood purges our conscious from dead works by the eternal Spirit so that we can serve the living God (see Hebrews 9:14).

GOD WILL NEVER GET RID OF WHAT YOU SHOULD KEEP

Looking at this verse causes me to think about my own conscience and realize that it, too, needs to be purged, for I also have many dead works. God tells us just how He will do the purging. So when He reveals His good Word to you, yield and let the blood of Christ, by His eternal Spirit, do any purging work needed in your conscience.

Believe me, God will never get rid of what you should keep or have. Although I barely know, yet He always knows what's best and good and right for you and me, and I'm learning to trust Him in this. This trust for God has grown little by little, to be sure. Actually, I remember the day faith included trust. For on that day I had a one-way conversation with myself, saying, "God, I don't know anything about Your kind of wisdom, and I only know what I know." But I was willing to know His. Also, I was willing to trust His wisdom over my own.

So, here again, a choice, a decision, was made on my part, and so the beginnings of trust occurred right then and there, plus more letting go of myself, making room for more of God.

No Church Can Save You

How about you? What do you trust in? Is it more in yourself than God? Of course, it's okay to be where you are, but this is just to let you know that there is also trust to have, as well as faith. And, by the way, if you think that because you go to church that will save you, you're mistaken. Perhaps it's understandable that you think it should be so, but unless you truly believe that Jesus Christ is the Son of God and have confessed Him, you cannot be saved. Saint Paul taught the Roman believers:

> *If thou shalt confess with thy mouth the Lord Jesus, and shalt believe in thine heart that God hath raised him from the dead, thou shalt be saved. For with the heart man believeth unto righteousness; and with the mouth confession is made unto salvation. For the scripture saith, Whosoever believeth on him shall not be ashamed. For*

there is no difference between the Jew and the Greek: for the same Lord over all is rich unto all that call upon him. For whosoever shall call upon the name of the Lord shall be saved. Romans 10:9-13

Your salvation simply will not happen unless you do this, and if you fail to do it, you will have "missed it" because you heard the truth and put it off, or even made fun of it. Choose to mock God at your own peril! He is real, Heaven is real, His Kingdom is real, the devil is real and so is Hell!

YOU STILL HAVE THE PRIVILEGE OF CHOICE

You still have the privilege of choice, and if you're still not sure, God has even made provision for your unbelief:

I believe; help thou mine unbelief. Mark 9:24

This was said in the context of a father seeking Jesus for his son to be healed, but it also shows me that God has even made a way for those who struggle with doubt. This man was honest with Jesus, and yet the Lord made a way for him.

So just tell Him what you are and what you're not. This is called confession, and it's a very good starting point. I know, for it was mine a long while ago, and by God's grace and mercy, it continues to be effective in my life today.

GET UP!

So, dear reader, although you may fall along the way, if you do, get up and go on. Take time to talk the matter over with God, find out where you missed it or "blew it," as we say these days, and find out what can be done about it.

Maybe you just need to ask God for another opportunity. The toddlers around you are a good example. They fall many times, but they just keep on getting up and going on. Yes, sometimes they hurt themselves. They cry a little and are "bothered," and you may be too. That's okay. Just don't stay in that state any longer then you absolutely must. Otherwise, you might risk falling into a "pity party," and you can't afford to do that. Besides, it's not good for you.

Always remember, when you fall, that Jesus is not out to condemn you, so you should refrain from condemning yourself. Just avail yourself of His grace, which is always there to help you in your time of need. Rather than condemn you, He wants to comfort you. He is the Comforter. He said to His disciples:

> *I will pray the Father, and he shall give you another Comforter, that he may abide with you for ever.*
>
> John 14:16

If the Holy Spirit was *"another Comforter,"* then Jesus must have been the original Comforter. Take the comfort offered to you by Jesus and the Holy Spirit.

Since He is the Comforter, then it's not wrong to seek His comfort. If this was not available to you, why would Jesus have said it? He really does it, so take advantage of this blessing, which is the work of God on your behalf.

THE HOLY GHOST IS OUR TEACHER

The Holy Ghost is also our teacher:

> *But the Comforter, which is the Holy Ghost, whom the Father will send in my name, he shall teach you all things, and bring all things to your remembrance, whatsoever I have said unto you.*
>
> John 14:26

"Well, if You're the Teacher, then I must be the pupil!"

When I first read in the Bible that the Holy Ghost was our Teacher, it caused me to stop and think. I still remember the moment. I was alone at the dining room table reading the Bible, and when I read those words, I stopped and said, "Well, if You're the Teacher, then I must be the pupil. Whatever You want me to know, I'll be happy to learn." And God, by His precious Holy Spirit, has been teaching me from the Bible ever since.

The Holy Spirit also brings back to my memory things God has said in His Word. It's rather like an elevator going to the top floor. In this case, it's with my thoughts. That's "neat," isn't it?

I must say that I surely do depend upon God's Spirit to continue to teach me. I need it, and He said He would do it, so He will. God's Holy Spirit is a great gift from the Father to us. God knows that we surely need His presence with us, and we must not discount or dismiss Him from this journey we are called to take.

He Will Help Us in Other Ways Too

He will help us in other ways too. One evening I was in the kitchen, cleaning up after a meal, and I overheard a conversation in the other room that was very upsetting to me. I didn't want to say anything, for I was learning to hold my peace (not an easy thing for me). I certainly didn't want to get angry and say something I shouldn't say.

I stood with my hands on the edge of the kitchen counter, feeling my emotions quickly rising, and, at the same time, praying, "God, I don't want to become angry. Please help me with my emotions." And when I said that, immediately my upset emotions just totally stopped. Wow!

I wondered, What just happened to me? All I could think to compare it with was a balloon being pricked with a pin and instantly deflating. I was so glad that God had helped me. Surely I could not help myself in this situation, and I knew it. He helped me not to fall into the trap of saying the wrong things and doing the wrong things.

So, know that His help and comfort can be there for you whenever necessary. They are but a prayer away. And if you want to be taught of the Lord, there is no shortage of lessons He can use to help you learn His truths. The important thing always is not just to know what is right, but to act upon it. If you're not sure, ask Him to make it plain to you, and He will. Wouldn't you do that for your child?

A SOURCE OF WISDOM

The Bible is a source of wisdom that can keep you from falling. For example, I love the book of Proverbs. For those who are new to the Bible, this book is located in the Old Testament right after the book of Psalms. Take a look at Proverbs, and you'll see all the "goodies," the insights and the wisdom, that God so freely offers each of us there.

This book speaks of God's Spirit granting wisdom, knowledge and understanding to all those who will seek Him for it. I need more of all three. Of late, I've had to seek Him especially for more understanding.

Recently I discovered in the Bible that God can also give us quick understanding, and, as you might have already guessed, I'm asking Him for that too. I need it.

Let me add something here, and that is: do try to measure your words and thoughts by what God says in His Word. When something doesn't line up with His Word, dismiss it quickly. Why? So that you don't get tripped up and fall when you don't have to, as you journey along with Him in this, His good earth.

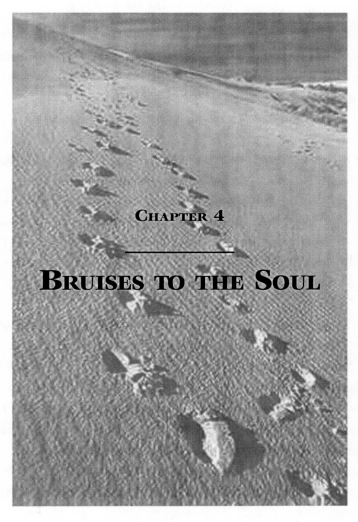

CHAPTER 4

BRUISES TO THE SOUL

And Jesus went about all Galilee, teaching in their syna-
gogues, and preaching the gospel of the kingdom, and
healing all manner of sickness and all manner of dis-
ease among the people. Matthew 4:23

I have come to love and enjoy God's thoughts. He
does have thoughts, and they are nothing like you might

think. The thoughts He shares with me are short, distinct and to the point. After all, He knows what we need to hear. Oh, what a mighty God our heavenly Father is!

GOD SPEAKS TO US THROUGH HIS SON

God speaks in many ways. First, He speaks to us through Jesus, His only begotten Son. This truth is spelled out in the first chapter of the book of Hebrews. I would encourage you to read its words out loud, even if there are others around. Give them a chance to also hear what God is saying in His Word. Surely these words are life and truth to all who find them:

> *God, who at sundry times and in divers manners spake in time past unto the fathers by the prophets, hath in these last days spoken unto us by his Son, whom he hath appointed heir of all things, by whom also he made the worlds; who being the brightness of his glory, and the express image of his person, and upholding all things by the word of his power, when he had by himself purged our sins, sat down on the right hand of the Majesty on high; being made so much better than the angels, as he hath by inheritance obtained a more excellent name than they.*
> *For unto which of the angels said he at any time, Thou art my Son, this day have I begotten thee? And again, I will be to him a Father, and he shall be to me a Son? And again, when he bringeth in the first begotten into the world, he saith, And let all the angels of God worship him.* Hebrews 1:1-6

So, what did you hear? What did you learn? Let me break it down a little. This is what I do for myself:

- God speaks to us by His Son (who is Jesus, the Christ).
- His Son is heir of all things.
- His Son made all the worlds.
- His Son is the image of God.
- His Son upholds all things by the word of His power.
- His Son purged our sins.
- His Son sat down at the right hand of the Majesty on high.
- His Son is so much better than the angels.
- His Son has obtained, by inheritance, a more excellent name.
- God is a Father to Jesus, and Jesus is a Son to Him.
- All the angels of God are to worship the Son.

When you let God speak to you in this way, something from His Word will click with you, and it will also stick with you!

Too detailed? Maybe, but I wanted you to see how you can think on what God says in a little slower way, so as to get something from it that you can take to heart. When you let God speak to you in this way, something from His Word will click with you, and, because of that, it will also stick with you.

For me, what clicks, as I write this, is that Son of God made all the worlds. That now makes me more interested in the planets and makes me want to talk about them with God and ask Him all kinds of questions. His responses, of course, will be found somewhere in the Bible. And they, in turn, will cause me to go on to other truths.

READING THE BIBLE IS FUN AND EXCITING

Reading the Bible can be a lot of fun and very interesting, besides being enlightening. Everything I read gives me more to talk to God about.

At first (and for a very long time), the only things I talked with God about were the problems I was facing in life, my personal lacks and faults and, yes, my sins. But He, over time, along with many teachings, caused my personal growth to steadily progress. He forgave me much and healed me much, and so many of the things that bothered me before were dealt with and resolved. Now, therefore, I'm able to speak with Him about other things.

A SCAVENGER HUNT

I think of studying God's Word a little like a scavenger hunt. We are going from place to place, gathering all that relates to a given subject. We start at one place in His Word and move along to another and another, and we do this until we are finished in one of two ways: (1) We end up right back where we started, for we've come full circle. Or (2) We're fully satisfied, as with eating a good meal, and we stop for the moment—even though we still want more. Discovering the truths of God's Word is just that "neat."

Would you like this journey to begin for you? It's never boring, for it's always new. The "kicker," if I may say it that way, is that being with God reminds me of watching a sunset. It's always beautiful and never the same twice. You can read the very same verse at some later time, and God will reveal even more to you through it by His Spirit.

How wonderful is that? God is so vast—so big! No wonder we have the promise of eternity with Him! I'm going to need it. How about you?

THIS BOOK IS FOR YOU

Speaking about you, let me be bold for a moment. God, the Father of Jesus Christ, would have you to know that one of the reasons this book has been written is just for you. Why? Because He wants you to spend eternity with Him and His Son Jesus. Since He has been removed from our American public school system, He is all too aware of the fact that you may not know about Him, and since so many mock Him, make sport of Him and use His

God wants you to make a choice to believe and receive His Son, Jesus, and in doing so, to receive His gift of life!

name in a degrading way, you may have formed some erroneous impressions of Him.

I could continue on, but I think you get the point. God wants you to make a choice to believe and receive His Son, Jesus, and in doing so, to receive His gift of life. As noted earlier, Jesus said:

I am come that they might have life, and that they might have it more abundantly.   John 10:10

If this is not the day, then there will come a day when Jesus will someway and somehow come and knock at the door of your heart and ask you to let Him in. In the last book of the Bible, He said:

Behold, I stand at the door, and knock: if any man hear my voice, and open the door, I will come in to him, and will sup with him, and he with me.   Revelation 3:20

So you have a choice to make: believe God about His Son Jesus and receive the new life

He offers. If you do that, you can become *"a new creature"*:

> *Therefore if any man be in Christ, he is a new creature: old things are passed away; behold, all things are become new.*   2 Corinthians 5:17

How can you do this? Well, when Christ is knocking on the door of your heart, you must respond. Just open the door to your heart and life and say, "Yes, come in and be my Lord." With that simple invitation, He will come in.

If you're like me, always apologizing for the way you or your house look, go ahead and do that with Jesus, but He will not condemn you. Instead, He will forgive and cleanse you.

Then comes the journey with Christ Jesus and His Holy Spirit, a journey in which you move along as you are, having God moments, gaining new insights into the new paths you're on. At one point, I had a change of direction without looking for one.

WHAT NEVER CHANGES?

I was always a very conscientious mother, wanting what was right and good for my children at all times, but even though I had great love for them, I knew that I was lacking "big time" as a mother. I didn't always know what to do, nor how to do it, so I read women's magazines in an attempt to learn as much as I could. One day, as I was reading a particular article in one of those magazines, it dawned on me that what was being said in that article was just the opposite of what had been said in previous articles. It was what I have often called a flip-flop. Now it is, and now it's not, and, instead, this is the new reality.

I immediately stopped reading and just sat there wondering: Now, what am I to do? Here's a person with letters behind his name, a man who is considered to be "learned" in his field. Is this what experts do, change their minds every few years as the tide of public opinion changes? Who and what can I depend on? That moment a search began within me, a search for something that would never change. I kept thinking over and over, "What has not changed? What will never change?"

I was still sitting there on that small, black rocking chair, that had once belonged to my husband's grandmother, and I was still rocking, but my mind was elsewhere. It was moving like a computer, searching, searching, searching ... until, suddenly, I knew the answer. I knew exactly what would never change. It was the Bible.

As I continued to rock and think on this, I then made a decision within myself, which was, this would be the last time I looked to another source for the mothering help I needed to raise my children. From that moment on, I would look to the Bible and what God had to say. I could trust it to be real and unchanging, when nothing else was.

SOMETHING MORE STABLE

How about you? Are you looking for something more stable in life, something more dependable, more sure and completely trustworthy? Well, dear reader, there is indeed something just like that, and it's called the Bible. This sacred book has been around for many centuries now, and it will always be around.

For me, this was the beginning of going to the Bible, God's Word, for what to do and how to do it for raising my children. Did I do everything perfectly? Surely not. Ask my now-grown children, and they'll tell you. So does that mean that God missed it? No! Not at all! Although I continued wanting and seeking God, the truth was that my soul was "a mess." It was bruised, hurt, damaged, and all of this without me consciously knowing it.

ONLY GOD CAN HEAL THE SOUL

What is a soul? Simply said, your soul is your mind, will and emotions. We often get so busy with the details of living and tending to all that's needed to sustain life that we don't have time for our own soul. When our body hurts in some way, we make time to go to the doctor and get help. Usually, the doctor writes us a prescription, and we're on our way. In time, the sickness either passes or is masked over, and we go on living. But with the soul, this is not so easily done.

That is, until I heard at church one Sunday that only God can heal the soul and that in order for it to happen, we need to forgive those who have hurt us in the past. That word, that only God can heal the soul, so impacted me that I hardly heard the rest of the message. As I got into my car to go home that day, I found that I didn't want to leave the place. I needed to talk with God—right then and there—about this matter.

I kept thinking of the need for forgiving a person who had hurt me some years before. I thought I had forgiven them, so I said to God, "I was sure I had forgiven them, but, for some reason, those words they spoke and the wounds they caused still hurt." These words had come back to me from time to time, and I would wonder why—when I thought I had forgiven the person.

Having heard the words, "only God can heal a soul," now caused me to realize that, although I had truly forgiven the person, still there was something else going on inside of me. There was some sort of lingering affect from the unkind words this person had spoken to me. Those words had wounded my soul, and that wound had remained in me, unseen by others, and even worse, unseen by me. I was seriously wounded, and yet I hadn't even been conscious of that fact. Thankfully, God was. He even made a way for me to be healed. And it started with His spoken Word. See how important it is to think over what you hear from a man of God, someone whom God uses to bring it forth!

DOES YOUR SOUL NEED HEALING?

How about you, dear reader? Does this bring something to your mind? Have you experienced words that deeply hurt you? And have they been lodged there in your soul, festering for a long time now?

It may have been more than bad words that damaged your soul. Bad acts may have been committed against you, and your soul suffered bruising as a result. If so, please let this be a beginning of complete healing for you.

Whatever happened to you in the past, talk it over with the Lord Jesus, and let Him touch you and heal you. Stay with Him until quietness and peace come from His Spirit to yours.

THE POWER OF WORDS

Let me digress here for a moment and emphasize how very powerful our words are. Please be careful with the words you speak to others. Why? Many still don't know that there is *"death and life"* in the tongue (Proverbs 18:21). Words can pierce and even alter a life for the better, but they can also alter a life for the worse.

Words are very much like seeds. They can take root

> *"I was sure I had forgiven them, but, for some reason, those words they spoke and the wounds they caused still hurt!"*

and bring forth fruit—good fruit or bad fruit. This is so important that I could go on with this subject for a while. Please give this point some serious thought, as we need to move on.

GOD MINISTERED HEALING TO MY SOUL

So what was it that was said to me that left my soul in need of healing? God knew, and right there in my car He ministered healing to my soul. Only He sees the heart and the soul, and only He is all wise and all knowing. I'm so glad not to be left to myself with life's limited resources.

There in my car I cried out to God, "Only You can heal a soul. Lord Jesus, I know that I forgave this person, but now I realize that what has bothered me off and on through the years has been the wounds left by the words they spoke. I'm looking to You to heal my soul today."

I had nothing more to say, but it was enough. In the quietness of my car, my God, through His wonderful Son Jesus, healed my soul. How He did it I really don't know, but He did it, and He did it right then and there.

HOW DID I KNOW?

How can I know that I was healed? Some time later, I had another recall of that particular incident, but this time the hurt and the wound did not rise to the surface. It was totally gone, and in its place was complete quietness.

Since that time, the word *soul* has meant a lot to me, and I find it here and there throughout the Bible, especially the book of Psalms. Whenever I see this word in the Bible, I stop and look to see and learn and come to know what more God has to say about our souls. Let me encourage you to taste and see for yourself that God's Word is ever so good.

Through this experience, I have come to know and believe that although our body needs attention and healing, the soul needs it much more. Please don't neglect your soul.

Again, please talk this over with the Lord Jesus, and let Him touch you and minister to you. Stay with Him until a quietness and peace comes from His Spirit to yours. Why? For truly, only God can heal the bruises and other damages done to your soul. He has done it for me, sometimes quickly and sometimes through a process, and surely, since He is no respecter of persons, He can and will do it for you, too.

DON'T PUT IT OFF

So I encourage you to take advantage of the divine moments when God is ready to make it happen. Whether you are in a car, sitting in a chair at home, at church or even in your bathroom, just stop and take the time to be with Him. Why? To receive a refreshing or the much needed healing of your souls' bruises or wounds.

In these moments, don't just concentrate on what you might consider to be a "biggie." Let this great and almighty God and Father do all that He desires to do in and for your soul.

Please, don't put this matter off. It's too important. When God is speaking to you, that's your God-ordained moment in time. And it may well be a case of "now or never." Why? Although there are many reasons, one important one is that you cannot make this happen yourself. Only God can. Respond when He speaks to you, for you surely don't want to miss this opportunity. 🌾

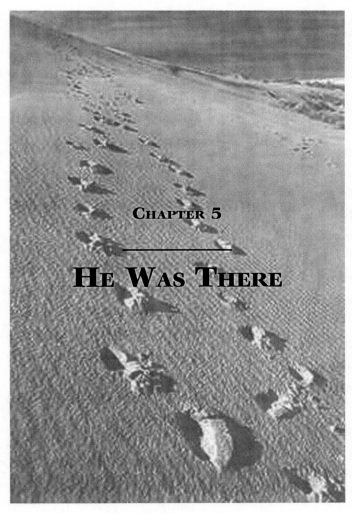

CHAPTER 5

HE WAS THERE

For the invisible things of him from the creation of the world are clearly seen, being understood by the things that are made, even his eternal power and Godhead; so that they are without excuse. Romans 1:20

I was recently thinking about what we see of airplanes from the ground. They steadily climb higher and higher into the sky, and it's so "neat" to watch them from below—until you finally lose sight of them. Then, it's all blue sky and clouds, for the plane has disappeared from sight.

But the flight has not stopped. It continues, as the pilot guides the plane even higher, way up above the clouds, above the existing weather patterns and beyond our sight.

> *Creation needs all kinds of weather to keep everything in balance. And, besides, it smells so good after a rain!*

You may be wondering exactly what I'm getting at. Well, likening our journey to the flight of an airplane, I realize that God has also caused me to rise above the weather as well. Now overcast or rainy days no longer bother me. And like that airplane, even though I cannot see Him, God is always there.

THE SUN IS ALWAYS THERE

Years ago, I was in my car one day heading back home after delivering early morning newspapers, and all I could see along the horizon were gray clouds. The sun was nowhere to be seen, and that really bothered me. Why? I missed it, and, even more, I missed God. I was not sensing His presence because of the gloominess of the day.

Then, as I continued to drive along, I began thinking, The sun must be there. How could it be otherwise? Suddenly it dawned on me that the sun was always present—whether I could see it or not. Clouds had covered it and obscured it from my view, but it was still there.

This may seem corny or "goofy" to some, but that simple realization caused me to become contented and at peace that day. I was at peace with creation. Creation needs all kinds of weather to keep everything in balance. And, besides, it smells so good after a rain.

Then came another, equally powerful, realization: God is always present with us, even though He, like the sun, can be hidden at times. Even if He doesn't show Himself, that doesn't mean that He's gone away. He's always there.

New Seasons Come Gradually

Have you noticed that when a new season comes and an old one goes, the transition into the next is gradual? The old ends gradually, and the new begins gradually, until the old is gone and the new has taken over. God eases us into the next season. Isn't He so "neat" in the way He does things?

He is so kind, so gentle and so peaceable. He is not at all abrupt, although He can and will do things suddenly.

There's a difference. When things are done abruptly, there's a certain yanking or a sudden disturbance, and there's never any good that comes of it. As we have noted, for the most part, God gets all the blame for the bad things that happen in the world. This is very sad because He was there all the time, trying to give you the help you needed. You just didn't recognize His nudge.

Let me explain this a bit better. I have a wonderful friend named Mollie, and Mollie has told me about what she calls "God-nudges." What she means by this is that when something is going on in your life, it may be God nudging you to do His will. By His Spirit, He nudges you to do something, and He also nudges you about things not to do. This is His way of preventing what would not be good for you or of moving you to do what you have thought about but not yet acted upon.

EXAMPLES OF COMMON GOD-NUDGES

Here are some examples. While you're in the checkout line at the supermarket, you think about going back to get some eggs, but you reason it away, saying to yourself, "I don't need them; I have enough." Then, a couple of days later, when you're in the middle of baking, you suddenly find yourself one egg short, and you have to stop what you're doing and go to the store. You could have had enough on hand—if you had known to pay attention to the Lord's nudges.

Or, how about when you're out visiting some garage sales in the neighborhood, and twice the thought crosses your mind to stop and go home, but you decide to visit just one more house. What you don't know (but God does) is that there's a raised sidewalk ahead that you're about to trip over. Instead of having the fall prevented by giving heed to the nudges of the Holy Spirit, you now fall flat. Thankfully, you suffer only scrapes, but your eyeglass frames will need repair. (It happened to me.)

You're on the highway, and you have recurring thoughts (Holy Spirit nudges, really), to take a different route. Instead, you continue on your current course. You don't know that a detour has been recently placed into affect in that area, and now you will be delayed. Too late you realize that you should have listened.

You're God-nudged to get some gas. Later will be fine, you think to yourself, but "later" proves to be too late.

YOUR OWN GOD-NUDGES

Most of us have experienced this type of continuing nudges to go to a certain place or to attend a certain event, but we talk ourselves out of it with our usual excuses: "I'm too tired" or "I don't feel like it." Later, when you find out just how good the event was, then you're kicking yourself for not going. I suppose we could all fill many pages with examples of such God-thoughts or God-nudges that we missed, dismissed or even overrode. The resulting losses are always tragic because God has sent the Holy Spirit to help us, to comfort us, to enable us and, yes, also to remind us.

Just as parents need to remind a child of something they let slip, fail to give heed to or just don't pay enough attention to, we adults also need help in this area. God knows this and surely has provided for it. But it's always up to us to believe, yield and receive.

"Blowing It" and Putting God Off

Recently I was reminded about the importance of such God-nudges, and I realized that, all too often, I was "blowing it" with God and I confessed to Him that I was doing so and how sorry I was.

Always take the time to admit and confess to God your wrongs and mistakes. He can make good out of them or even give you another chance. Yes, I have to admit that confessing our wrongs is not pleasurable, but we can get used to eating humble pie. I know, for I have surely eaten my share. (I much prefer blueberry.)

Later that same day, God gave me another revelation. He caused me to know something else, and it was that I was putting Him off. Let me repeat that again. I was putting God off!

It wasn't that I didn't want to do what God was calling me to do. Rather, it was the fact that I was in the middle of doing something else and didn't want to stop what I was doing. Because of this, I was treating His nudges as something to add to a mental list of things to do "later." But every God-given nudge is to be acted upon, and many times it must be acted upon immediately—not later.

Such acts of God's Holy Spirit are meant for our good or for someone else. When we always wait until "later," the thing God is telling us to do usually gets forgotten or, worse, it's too late by the time we get ready to obey. We've all experienced it.

So, if you keep thinking to do a good thing, do let yourself be interrupted. If you keep thinking to call a person (or whatever else), then do it. Whatever God wants, let Him have his right of way. Why? Because the God of all creation, Christ Jesus, should have His way. Simply stop and do what He is nudging you to do. And I'm saying this to myself as well.

God Is Everywhere

So, as you can see, God is here, and He is there. He is indeed everywhere, and I'm sincere in saying that He is far more than many seem to know. He is there when someone offers you a helping hand or when another gives you a smile. He is there when your neighbor snow blows your driveway or when someone gives you a meal. He is there when you think you're alone or when you think no one cares. If you're like me, maybe you'll come to know later on that God was really there all the time. And yes, He is there for you today, even right now, this very moment. ❧

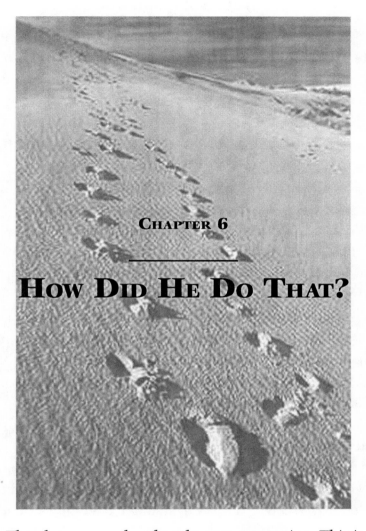

CHAPTER 6

HOW DID HE DO THAT?

Then he answered and spake unto me, saying, This is
the word of the LORD unto Zerubbabel, saying, Not by
might, nor by power, but by my spirit, saith the LORD
of hosts. Zechariah 4:6

How did He do that? I find this to be an interesting
title and also a bit tough to write about. "Why?" you may

ask. Because it's not pleasurable to share your faults, mistakes, errors and also what the Bible calls *"iniquities"* (Psalm 38:4). But if I failed to do this, I would be doing you a disservice. So, with that said, here goes.

MANY THINGS CARRY OVER INTO OUR NEW LIFE

Having a sensitive nature carries over into our new life. Actually, most everything about us does. That includes the good, the not-so-good and (not to be left out) the bad. It also includes something that is not much heard about these days and much less spoken of: sin, the wrongs we do to ourselves, to others and to God.

Well, isn't this a mouthful to take in and then to try to digest? But you can digest it. For me, humor seems to help. It breaks up or cuts into the tension built up within me. If you find you are short on humor, why not ask God for some? I did, and He gave it to me.

Was I worthy or deserving of this favor? Surely not. And where was I to get the humor I needed? Well, God has everything, so this is no problem for Him.

God will do anything and everything for us, and this includes correcting us, or chastising us, when we need it.

THE LORD KNOWS WHEN WE NEED CORRECTION

The first time this happened to me, I somehow knew it was coming (just as a child does), and I was uneasy about it. I said, "You know, God, that I can't stand pain, so could You please make this quick?" The humor helped, and God corrected and loved me at the same time. Recalling it now, the correction seemed to be over rather quickly.

Lessons Learned

As I continue on, I must say that although I am not an ordained minister or a person with college degrees, still God has chosen me to share what I've come to learn and know, along with some life experiences.

Speaking of experience, some can really be likened to a lesson. At times, when my then teenagers were telling me of something going on that they didn't like, I would ask them, "So, what are you learning from this? Although they waited patiently for me to run out of words, still they didn't like to hear this question. Why am I saying this to you? Because it is really a good question to consider, as a lot can be learned from whatever is happening in our lives.

> *Speaking of experience, some can be likened to a lesson!*

For me, I truly believe that God knows everything, and when things are happening, I seek Him to understand what's going on. Sure, it takes time and effort to seek and find out in prayer, but you really can come to know. Granted, it won't be all, but surely it will be enough to satisfy you or give you peace of mind.

How you approach God will really matter. Do look at Philippians 4:6-7, for it would be a good way to pray. Recently God used those verses to teach me a little more on how to deal with worry. There He said, *"Be careful for nothing; but in every thing by prayer and supplication [crying out] with thanksgiving let your requests be made known unto God. And the peace of God, which passeth all understanding, shall keep your hearts and minds through Christ Jesus."*

After thinking that over for some minutes, I said, "How do you do that?"

Immediately God's thought was in my mind, which was, "What do you need?"

I immediately got up from the couch and went into the family room and stood in front of the old barber chair and did what Philippians 4:6 said. I presented my need, for it to go to its next home. I told God how thankful I was for all the fun times my children had with it while they played pool, but I felt that it was time for another family to enjoy it too.

In case you're wondering how I could have God's thoughts. Well, I ask for them all the time. Why? Because some time ago, I saw in Philippians 2:5, this good word, *"Let this mind be in you, which was also in Christ Jesus."* I said, "God I do want the mind of Christ, and I do let it be in me." For me getting thoughts and understanding from God is so helpful and even very much needed. It causes me to hold steady and keep standing in spite of what I don't like or can't change or control.

Sometimes there are a lot of experiences or circumstances that happen that will pull and tug on and at your faith, even put great strain on it. Plus, there can be a stretching or inner growth going on while you are in your situation. And that stretching can be good, although it certainly may not seem so at the time.

Never Give Up on Your Faith

Please never give up on your faith in God because of anyone or any thing. I know that this is easier said than done. There are times of testing for your faith through unseen circumstances, but you can hold on, especially when you consider the thought: there could be something in this whole situation that you don't yet understand. So please don't cast your faith aside, even if you momentarily want to or are being tempted to do so. Remember, there is a lot going on in the spirit that you may not understand yet.

Have you ever noticed that when you answer a child's question, "why?," it just causes them to have more whys? After a while you realize that nothing you can say will satisfy them. Could that be the reason that some of our questions to God seem to go unanswered? Just a thought!

Recognize that your faith is a treasure. Value it, even when it seems to diminish, for it is worth more than gold and silver. Never let it go. Stop being angry with God (if you are), or worse yet, never curse God, for He is love.

Yes, God is love and truth, and He cannot lie. There's a lot we don't yet know, or maybe we're not yet ready to know. First comes the milk, and then the meat of the

Word (see Hebrews 5:12-13 and 1 Peter 2:2). At other times, we can know what's going on and learn to deal with it. I had a testing, a growing of my faith, a real learning lesson that may be of help to others.

> *I quieted myself down inside and confessed to God that I was sorry for how I had acted and spoken!*

I WAS ANGRY WITH GOD

One day I got very angry with God. I was upset and discouraged, and I openly expressed to Him my thoughts and feelings. The reason for all of this was that my twin brother Jim had been held for some time in the county jail, that day he had suffered through yet another courtroom hearing and was told once again by the same judge to come back the next month. When this had happened the month before, his court-appointed lawyer had said he would most likely be home after the next hearing. Now, that hearing, too, had passed, and there was yet another delay. My brother wasn't going home with me, and I was "bugged" and "bothered" about it.

As I drove home from the hearing that day alone, I was expressing my displeasure to God. Why? Because I had gone without food, fasting and praying (praying a lot and very sincerely) for my bother's release. And yet what I thought would happen that day, what I was believing God for, had not come to pass.

In the midst of my distress over this personal setback, I remembered a time years before when I had been angry with God, and the results had not been good. "It's not good to be angry with God," I reminded myself.

On that earlier occasion, God had used the teachings of Job 38:1-42:3 to correct me "royally." His Word set me straight that time, and I knew that I could not afford to ignore this hard-learned lesson.

Just as with our natural children, we need to know where our boundary line is with God and then be careful not to cross it. Charging God or complaining about His actions isn't a wise thing to do ever. Coming and reasoning together with Him certainly is (see Isaiah 1:18).

I Quieted Myself

With these thoughts in mind, I quieted myself down inside and confessed to God that I was sorry for how I had acted and spoken. Fortunately, I didn't give up on prayer and talking things over with God about my twin brother. One conversation went like this: "God, I don't know if he's guilty or not." It seemed to me that things could go either way, and I didn't want to get in the way of the outcome by praying wrong. So I simply prayed, "You, God, know fully what happened, and if he needs to be in jail, then okay. If not, then that shouldn't be."

I must note here that, for the most part, I usually don't know what to pray for and have to ask God to help me know what and how to pray. He is faithful, and, by His Spirit, He leads me to something in the Bible. And that's what I pray for.

Why am I sharing this? Because I had failed to do this for my brother. For the first few months of his ordeal, I had just been praying about what I saw and knew. That was good and effective ... until I got so "bugged" and "bothered" and wondered why my prayers were not being answered. I wasn't aware of it at the time, but the very next day I would find out the why of it all.

FINDING MY ANSWER THROUGH HIS FELLOWSHIP

You see, early each morning, when I came before God, I would begin by naming some things I was very thankful to Him for. This was what the Lord had taught me early on, and I stuck with it. I would actually hold up my fingers and use them to name off ten things I was thankful for. By the time I got to ten, I was becoming so thankful that I often continued on. This time of thanksgiving was something like a diving board. It helped me quickly get into the spiritual water. (And Jesus is that Living Water that we can get into and draw from.)

I didn't realize it at the time, but God's Spirit was teaching me the truth of the Psalms:

Enter into his gates with thanksgiving, and into his courts with praise.   Psalm 100:4

I simply took God at His Word, and all I know is that it worked for me. Worship prepares us to come before the King of kings and Lord of lords, Jesus Christ, in a way that is pleasing to Him.

READY FOR A CONVERSATION

Once I had completed my time of thanksgiving, I'd say, "It's Your show and Your good earth, so what do You want to talk about?" Why speak this way? Because this was not a time for prayer petitions or even a Bible study, though it could be. It was simply being one-on-one with God, for who He was and for whatever He wanted to say or do. Then, as the Spirit brought some scripture to my mind, that's where we began our discussion. At times, God used a page from a daily devotional book as a guide for what I was to think on, along with its Bible references.

This whole time is mostly personal. He uses it to bring about exactly what I need to hear and know. It may be encouraging scripture, coming to new knowledge or being corrected or instructed.

The process can take an hour. For me, time is not an issue because I'm up early enough to have it. Besides, like I said, God should have His time and His way and say. Don't you think? I must say, there are times when there were issues or situations that went on the day before that had left me upset. And try as I might, I could not work through or get past it. So then I would be coming before Him with issues or me needing to get straightened out first.

God is not rigid when this happens, as He can take and move me along when life is up for grabs, so to speak, and help me work it out. He then restores my peace, and I'm back on track.

LEARNING PRAISE

Praise words are not easy for me to say, and I do ask God to help me with that too. I remember, long ago, when I first heard someone say, "Praise God!" It sounded so foreign to me. I wondered, "What is that all about? And how can I say something I don't really mean?" I did not grow up with praise, so I struggled even with its meaning. But God, through His truth, has been in the process of setting me free. And, by the way, He can do that for you too. How? Go to John 8:31-32 and talk over whatever issues you have with God.

Although I am still learning to praise God, at times, praise and even worship comes at the end of this morning time, sometimes with a shout, maybe a song made up from my heart or a few words of scripture to sing that is brought to mind by the Holy Spirit. Sometimes there's a dance of joy and I always end praying the prayer of Jabez (see 1 Chronicles 4:10), plus, as I already mentioned, asking God to help me walk with Him and be a blessing.

Of course, you don't have to do what I do, but when He does call, do go and be with Him. Why? So you can hear what He has personally to say through His Word that will be just for you. Maybe this is a bit wordy, but please know that God is very interested in us all. He wants us to come to not only believe and receive from Him, but also to know Him in a personal way. And He very much desires to walk along with you in your life's journey.

The King's Heart Is in the Hand of the Lord

Now, I'd better get back to Jim's case, for my brother is a good example of God's care and love. The next morning God, by His wonderful Holy Spirit, led me to Proverbs. Let me share with you the verse He called to my attention that day:

> The king's heart is in the hand of the LORD, as rivers of water: he turneth it whithersoever he will.
>
> Proverbs 21:1

This caused me to stop and think deeply. I don't recall the whole process, but what I do recall is that God helped me to understand something very important that day. I was led to look up the word *king* in the dictionary, and as I read the definitions, things began going off in my mind.

Talking to God and meditating on His Word is a lot

Every single time the Spirit of God brought that verse to my mind, I immediately prayed it and decreed it!

103

like making popcorn. We let it sit over the heat for a while, and, at first, there seems to be little or no response. Then, suddenly, that corn begins to pop, and the popping gets faster and faster as the heat rises.

Suddenly, I got very happy, for I knew something that I had not known before. All the time I had been praying for my brother (and rightly so), there was someone else who needed my prayers. It was the one who was in charge, the authority who would eventually decide the outcome of the case.

The judge was the key to this case, and I suddenly knew that his heart was in the hand of God. That meant that God could change it. And that changed everything. I knew how to get the desired outcome.

THIRTY DAYS TO PRAY

My brother's next hearing would be in thirty days, and so for the next thirty days, I prayed Proverbs 21:1. This didn't mean that my very first prayer hadn't been heard. Not at all (see Daniel 10:12-14)! Although we can't see the battles going on in the heavenlies, such battles are being waged both for and against us. Paul wrote:

We wrestle not against flesh and blood, but against principalities, against powers, against the rulers of the darkness of this world, against spiritual wickedness in high places. Ephesians 6:12

During those thirty days, I didn't pray for God to turn

the judge's heart toward my brother. Not at all! What I prayed was for God to turn the judge's heart the way He wanted it to go. He always knows best.

I worked that verse in Proverbs as if I were kneading a piece of dough to make bread. Every single time the Spirit of God brought it to my mind, I immediately prayed it and decreed it (see Job 22:28). And I was still praying it as I drove to the next courtroom hearing.

It was only when I sat down in what looked like a church pew in that court room that I knew I was done praying. Now it was up to the King of kings to move (although I didn't know this at the time). Still, God did an amazing thing.

The Courtroom Was Nearly Empty

As the proceedings were called to order that day (in a different courtroom), there was a totally different judge in charge. There was also a totally different prosecutor (the assistant). Aside from the judge, the prosecutor, a reporter, my brother, his court-appointed attorney and a guard at the door, I was the only other person present. The courtroom was nearly empty.

The judge began by asking the prosecutor to tell him about the case. His response was odd. Although he had my brother's file in front of him on the table, he said, "I'm sorry judge, but I don't know anything about it."

The judge then addressed Jim directly, "Come up here," he said, "and tell me your side of the story." To me, that was a wonderful moment. At other court hearings, I had often thought, Why don't they let Jim tell his side of the story? Now, that was about to happen, and I was very happy about it.

> *If, until now, you haven't wanted to know Him or know what He thinks and says, you might want to rethink your position!*

IS THAT ALL?

What Jim had to say that day was short and to the point (he's nothing like his twin sister). When he had finished, the judge asked, "Is that all?"

Jim said simply, "Yes."

The judge next asked Jim's court-appointed defender what she wanted the outcome of this hearing to be. She stated her goal. He then gave the same opportunity to the prosecutor to see what he wanted the outcome to be. When he had listened to both sides, he quickly ruled in Jim's favor. My brother would spend a little more time in jail, but he would not go to prison. He was soon out and continuing his journey with God that had begun while he was in that jail (with plenty of time on his hands to think and pray).

A footnote to that story is this: As I left the courtroom that day, the police officer guarding the door said to me, "Your brother was really lucky. That was 'the hanging judge'!" The reality of this impacted me very deeply. I had seen firsthand how God could turn the heart of a king (the judge, in this case).

GIVE GOD A CHANCE

I would encourage you to give God a chance to show you what and how to pray, particularly for those in authority in your life—your town, your city and your state. This would include teachers, other school officials, government agents, members of Congress and Supreme Court judges, but it would also include priests, pastors and your boss at work. Just talking about and criticizing others, and thus venting steam, may help you express your frustrations, but bringing situations and people before the Lord in prayer is the better way to go. If that were not true, why would God tell us to do it?

I exhort therefore, that, first of all, supplications, prayers, intercessions, and giving of thanks, be made for all men; for kings, and for all that are in authority; that we may lead a quiet and peaceable life in all godliness and honesty. For this is good and acceptable in the sight of God our Saviour; who will have all men to be saved, and to come unto the knowledge of the truth.
1 Timothy 2:1-4

This is the way we can have peace in our personal lives and in the life of our nation, so please do what God says here. You'll be amazed at what He does because of your prayers.

And just think what might happen if we fail in this regard. This command is just as important today as it was some two thousand years ago in Timothy's time.

LAYING BRICKS

Prayer and the results it brings are so amazing to me. I look at praying as laying bricks. Each prayer is like adding another brick on top of those already laid. And God is the cement, holding it all together. I don't know about you, but surely He is holding me up and keeping me, more than I currently know—and probably even in spite of myself.

As I said before, usually I really don't know what to pray, so I ask God to help me, and He does. He does it by the Holy Spirit, the Spirit of Christ.

A PERFECT SACRIFICE

After all, God, our heavenly Father, did promise He would send us the Spirit. He was to come after Jesus died for you, me and all mankind. Why did He do that? A perfect sacrifice was required for our sins, and we have all sinned:

If we say that we have no sin, we deceive ourselves, and the truth is not in us.　　　　　1 John 1:8

If we say that we have not sinned, we make him a liar, and his word is not in us.　　　　1 John 1:10

I know that this may be tough to hear or take in, but you and I need to know this truth. We are sometimes presumptuous. Whenever I think of it, I pray the Psalm:

Keep back thy servant also from presumptuous sins; let them not have dominion over me: then shall I be upright, and I shall be innocent from the great transgression.   Psalm 19:13

Apparently presumption can happen, and God is using this Psalm to let us know so we can guard against it. The Holy Spirit is also called the Spirit of Truth, and He can lead us to the truth. If you want the truth about God, or anything else for that matter, ask Him. He said:

Ask, and it shall be given you; seek, and ye shall find; knock, and it shall be opened unto you: for every one that asketh receiveth; and he that seeketh findeth; and to him that knocketh it shall be opened.   Matthew 7:7-8

Loaded with Good Things

Actually, go back to chapter 5 of Matthew and read through chapter 7, for this entire section is loaded with good things that Jesus spoke when He was on earth, and He is still speaking them today. He is *"the same yesterday, and to-day, and for ever"* (Hebrews 13:8). If, until now, you haven't wanted to know Him or know what He thinks and says, you might want to rethink your position. As we have seen, entrance into Heaven will be granted through Him and Him alone.

On that day, He will either speak for you or He will speak against you. And that day will surely come.

His truth can set us free today:

Then said Jesus to those Jews which believed on him, If ye continue in my word, then are ye my disciples indeed; and ye shall know the truth, and the truth shall make you free. John 8:31-32

Do you want to know the truth and be set free? Then open your mouth and ask God for His help. Seek Him. Knock on His door. But don't be "bugged" or "bothered" if your answer doesn't come instantly. God can do things instantly, for He is still the Miracle Worker, but usually He does things in a process, moving you along one brick at a time. It's not a question of what God can do or not do; it's a question of what you can believe for and receive at the moment.

THIS IS GREEK TO ME!

When I first started reading the Bible, I began with the psalms. They were short, and I could relate (a little) to what they were saying. There was much more that I didn't "get," and that frustrated me. "God," I would say, "this is all Greek to me." Finally one day I'd had enough, and I said to Him, "God, I don't want to do it, but if You don't shine Your light brightly enough on this so that I can see what You're trying to show me, I'm about to 'chuck' this."

That was just my way. When things didn't work well, usually, after the third time, I would say, "Out you go!" I wasn't trying to challenge God, and I wasn't angry with Him. I was simply trying to understand, and not enough of what I was reading was making any sense to me.

I can't explain exactly what God did, but I can say that the very next time I read the Bible, something made sense to me. It happened the next time too, and has been happening ever since.

From then on, when I didn't understand something I was reading, I would say to God, "God, would you just 'fly it a little lower,'" and somehow it became clear. Or maybe I knew now to stop reading and come back to it the next day. I can't say for sure what happened. What I can say is that the next day, while I sat there reading and taking time to be with God, things began to make sense to me.

This is just my personal experi-

Jesus is not only the Door for the sheep, but I also see Him as a bridge! He helps me to cross over to Him, from unbelief to belief!

111

ence, and yours may be very different. The important point is to hold steady and talk to God, while reading His good Word, about what you're coming to know or are thinking about. It's so wonderful to be able to reason with Him and just be yourself.

STOP!

Stop whenever you discover something you hadn't previously known about God and enjoy the moment of the revelation or the inspiration. Once, when I was reading from Saint Paul's letter to the Colossian Christians, something hit my spirit. It said, like that portion from Hebrews we read in an earlier chapter, that everything was created by Jesus:

For by him were all things created, that are in heaven, and that are in earth, visible and invisible, whether they be thrones, or dominions, or principalities, or powers: all things were created by him, and for him: and he is before all things, and by him all things consist.
Colossians 1:16-17

I hadn't known this until that moment, and I was so "bowled over" by the thought that I stopped reading and said to the Lord, "You're really 'big stuff!' " His Word was feeding my soul.

From early childhood I went to church every Sunday, but it wasn't until I became born again and started to read and think about what the Bible said and to talk to God about it that I really came to know Him. Then I had to be fed. Giving a newborn two ounces of milk is plenty at first, but in order for them to keep on growing, they need a whole lot more. So finding out about Jesus being the Creator was, for me, a great revelation.

Our God is indeed great. He, Jesus Christ, is the King of kings and the Lord of lords, whether we believe it or not, and whether we like it or not. He is coming back again, and when He does *"every knee shall bow"* to Him:

> *For it is written, As I live, saith the Lord, every knee shall bow to me, and every tongue shall confess to God.*
>
> Romans 14:11

Every means every. Your knee will bow too—one way or another.

Get This Matter Settled

If you don't yet believe in this, the Christ, I encourage you to get this matter settled very soon. Talk over with Him your thoughts and even your doubts and whatever else you feel the need to discuss. Tell Him about your unbelief. If you say to Him, as that man in the Bible did, "Jesus, I believe, but help my unbelief," He'll do it. I know, for I have asked for that help too, and it was granted.

Jesus is not only the Door for the sheep, but I also see Him as a bridge. He helps me to cross over to Him, from unbelief to belief. How He does it I don't know, but He surely does.

If He's not responding or reacting to you as you want or expect, so what? He doesn't have to do what you want. Just hold steady and know that He'll respond in His own time and in His own way. Maybe you'll find yourself one day thinking and even saying, "How did He do that?"

GOD IS FUN

Truly God inspires. He really is a great God, full of surprises—and fun too. The best thing any of us can do is to get to know Him. When I first started in this journey with Him I remember saying, "You know, God. Why wait till I'm dead and in Heaven to know You? I'd rather get to know You now."

I know I'm going to Heaven, not because of my status or looks or good works. I know I don't deserve it. It's not because of a high IQ or anything else, for that matter. It's only because I have believed and received and confessed Jesus Christ, the only begotten Son of God. I confessed to Him my wrongdoings, and He

> *I look at my sins, wrongdoings, or whatever you want to call them, as being written on a blackboard, ready to be erased!*

became my Savior.

Then, after a while, He also became my Lord. I see Him, too, as King and Majesty, Friend and Brother. That's "big stuff." Wouldn't you say?

So how about you? Heaven and Hell will hold all types—rich and poor alike, the handsome and beautiful and those not so handsome or beautiful, the able and the not so able. I was probably the runt of my family, and that proves that God can save anyone.

I'm not just putting myself down. My siblings were smarter and brighter than me, and so are my children, but God and His Word truly transform. He has started a good work in me, and He will finish it. And that is a very happy thought for me.

Sound Doctrine

The Lord began His changes in me by renewing my mind with His good Word. Little by little, He transformed and turned me around, and in the process, He remolded me, teaching, correcting and constantly leading me along the way. This came, along with showing me His *"sound doctrine"* found in the Bible (Titus 2:1). And all the while God, who is love, was showing and giving me new mercy daily and grace upon grace.

In between, He showed me my wrongdoings and sin and gave me grace to perceive and confess them so I could be in line for the healing I so desperately needed. Thankfully, this all happened a little at a time. I don't think that most of us could bear a sudden transformation.

It might sound odd to some, but after a while, as God

115

was leading me to recognize some sin He already knew existed in me but that I had not yet discovered, the fact that I was seeing it for the first time made me happy. I knew that I would soon experience another healing. In fact, I was sure that it was right around the corner, for I had read the words of James:

> *Confess your faults one to another, and pray one for another, that ye may be healed.*   James 5:16

I knew I needed such healing, and so I and my prayer partner, who often came to recognize things at about the same time as I did, would confess to each other. We sometimes did this over the telephone. And then we would both confess to God, although most of my confession of sin was done directly to Him.

Not At All Pleasurable!

Was this baring of my soul somehow pleasurable? No! Not at all! But the end results were. So never shrink away from this process and go into denial or whatever other negative reaction might occur to you to have. God is preparing you to be part of His Bride, and that Bride must be without *"spot or wrinkle"* (Ephesians 5:27). There are sins in us that we are not aware of yet, but God will be faithful to reveal them to us.

I look at my sins, wrongdoings, or whatever you want to call them, as being written on a blackboard, ready to be erased. Only God can erase that board, but He can do it. He said that He would remove our sins from us *"as far is the east is from the west"*:

> *As far as the east is from the west, so far hath he removed our transgressions from us.*   Psalm 103:12

Amazingly, God even promises to forget our sins, when they're under the blood of Jesus:

> *I will forgive their iniquity, and I will remember their sin no more.*   Jeremiah 31:34

So whenever God brings something to my attention (through whatever method), I need to present myself before Him, not to beg, but to receive His extended forgiveness. If I'm willing to confess it all to Him, then the blood of Jesus Christ cleanses me from my sin.

How can I tell that God is cleansing me? Because of the tears that run down my face while I'm before Him.

The Importance of His Blood

It was so important and necessary for Jesus' blood to be shed. His precious blood cleanses me from the confessed sin and purges my conscience from dead works. Without His blood there could be no remission of sin (see Hebrews 9:22).

If you insist that you have no sin, then you're calling God a liar, so don't "hedge" on this. If your conscience or heart has become hardened, go get some of that humble pie I told you about. It will help soften a hardened heart.

God not only forgives us of our sins; He also cleanses us from all unrighteousness as well. If you want to get the full story on this truth, go to the back of the Bible, to Saint John's letter called 1 John, and start with chapter 1. Read slowly so that you can digest it better, and talk with Jesus and our heavenly Father along the way. Who knows, you may want a journey to begin, one that is just right for you. This is a journey to God and to love, for *"God is love"* (1 John 4:8 and 16).

Don't put God off when He draws you, as you cannot make this happen on your own. And don't be fooled into thinking that you have a lot of time. You may not have very much time at all.

Not Yet Finished

I thought I had finished this chapter, but then God began a work in me one morning, and I felt that He would have you to know about it. He really has a lot to say to us and a lot to do for us. If you want Him, you definitely can have Him in your life. I hope that what happened to me will be a blessing to you too.

As I was before the Lord one morning, immediately His word came to mind about being a *"new creature in Christ"*:

> *Therefore if any man be in Christ, he is a new creature: old things are passed away; behold, all things are become new.*   2 Corinthians 5:17

At the time, I wasn't sure where exactly this was located in the Bible, so I went to the concordance section, which shows words that appear frequently in the Bible and the most important passages they appear in. I looked up the word *new*, and one of the passages listed under it was this: *"all things become n.*, 2 Co. 5:17." That told me to turn to the second book of Corinthians and look in chapter 5 and verse 17. (At the beginning, I didn't know the Bible book abbreviations used in the concordance, but, in time, I learned them.)

Then I asked God to renew "a right spirit" within me!

I turned to 2 Corinthians 5:17, and after reading the complete verse, the word *new* still stuck out as being very interesting to me. At the right edge of the page, a reference number caught my eye, and I immediately jotted it down in my journal. It was #2582, referring to a topical heading. These topical headings show us where else a word has been used, and interestingly enough, the variety of meanings they sometimes convey. We can then use them to see what else God is saying on a given subject.

Nothing Seemed to Catch My Interest

Under that heading I went on to read five scripture passages relating to the term *new man*, but nothing seemed to catch my interest, so I moved on to the next topical heading. It was #2583. I started to read the verses listed there, but then my eye caught the heading numbered #2584. It was entitled "Strengthened and Renewed by the Holy Spirit." I read the first scripture passage under this heading. It was:

Create in me a clean heart, O God; and renew a right spirit within me. Psalm 51:10

Something in that passage caught my attention, and I went no further. Instead, I read and reread that verse, and when this happens, it always proves good for me. In the process, God, by His Holy Spirit, is gradually making that word become alive within me.

Now, I was thinking: Do I have *"a right spirit"* within me? And then I started talking to God about it, saying, "I know Your Spirit is fine, but do I have *'a right spirit'* in me?"

By the way, dear reader, this process is not instant and should not be rushed.

Do I Have "a Right Spirit"?

I decided to see what another translation of the Bible said in that particular verse, and I chose the version known as The Amplified Bible. This Bible was developed to give all of the possible meanings of a particular word or phrase used in the original Bible, so that we can get a better understanding of what God is saying. This is what the Amplified said for Psalm 51:10:

Create in me a clean heart, O God, and renew a right,
persevering, and steadfast spirit within me.

Bingo! Now God was getting me to the "nitty-gritty,"
so to speak, the heart of the matter. This was what He
wanted me to come to know. These words *persevering*
and *steadfast* just spoke or clicked with me.

I looked up the two words in a dictionary to make
sure of their meaning, and after reading about steadfast, I
thought, I'm not steadfast, but changing, and not constant, but wavering. So there it was—the moment to face
myself and do it before God.

I said, "God, You're such a wonder. You know everything there is to know about me, and yet You love me." I
went on talking to God about what I was and wasn't. I
told Him that I wanted to have *"a right spirit"* within me,
for I sensed that my spirit was not totally right.

I Confessed to God with Tears

Next I perceived that I should move from my desk to
the couch, and there I confessed with tears to God. He, in
turn, asked me if I would renounce Satan. I said that I
would. I didn't want anything to do with him. Then I
asked God to renew *"a right spirit"* within me.

Again, I don't know really how He does the things He
does within me, but He surely brought this to my attention. I hadn't known that my spirit wasn't right, and what
child seeks to be disciplined? What child says to his or
her parent, "Correct me. Show me where I am and where

I ought to be." No, we're usually off in "la-la land," busy with our own little thing, and sometimes we never even know that there is something much better awaiting us.

> *We're usually off in "la-la land," busy with our own little thing, and sometimes we never even know that there is something much better awaiting us!*

THE FLESH IS GOD'S ENEMY

Besides this, our flesh never wants to submit to God, for it's at odds with His Spirit. The apostle Paul had this to say to the Galatian believers of the first century church:

This I say then, Walk in the Spirit, and ye shall not fulfil the lust of the flesh. For the flesh lusteth against the Spirit, and the Spirit against the flesh: and these are contrary the one to the other: so that ye cannot do the things that ye would.   Galatians 5:16-17

If you continue studying this for yourself, you will find a clear description of what exactly the flesh is and what exactly the spirit is. I could take time and space to tell you here, but it's important for you to hear it from God directly.

Something else you should know is that a specific order is required by God. It is spirit first, then soul and lastly, the body. For far too many of us, it's the body first, then the soul and finally the spirit. The flesh always insists on being first.

The Flesh Is Never Satisfied

Have you noticed that the flesh or body is never really satisfied? It's a little like a young child, wanting its own way and crying and making a fuss if it can't have it.

What's a parent to do? Should they give in and give the child everything they cry for? Surely not, for that would constitute very poor training. Yes, it's a lot easier to give in to a child to have some peace and quiet, but if you do this too often, before long, that child will know how to "work" you. The end result will be that your growing child will be leading and training you, instead of the other way around. And that's what happens with our flesh when we constantly give in to it.

So if you want your life to get into God's kind of order, which brings a lot of joy and peace, He is ready to be a Father to you. Just ask Him what you need to do. All that He does is done out of love and care for us. He will surely love you, help you and guide you along in your journey with Him.

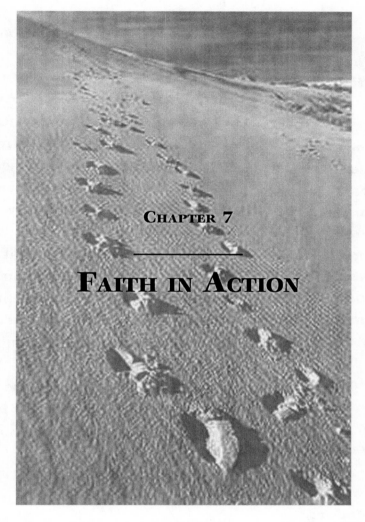

CHAPTER 7

FAITH IN ACTION

The just shall live by faith. Romans 1:17

What do we need faith for? Well, God tells us throughout the Bible, His Word, just how necessary this element called faith is. His Word on this subject has helped me, and I know it can help you too.

MUCH MORE THAN A BOOK

> *The Bible is a book, but it's much more than that. For me, it's a place I go where I find comfort, counsel, advice and, yes, correction!*

The Bible is a book, but it's much more than that. For me, it's a place I go where I find comfort, counsel, advice and, yes, correction. As we have noted, we need correction because we can be very sincere and, at the same time, very sincerely wrong.

The Bible shows us what is right and wrong from God's perspective, and that's the one that ultimately counts. The Bible helps me see and know where I am before God. And, if I want to be changed and grow, God, our heavenly Father uses His Word, by His Holy Spirit, to do the necessary work in me.

So is this hard or easy? Well, it's a little bit of both. Being transformed by the renewing of our minds through the Word of God was, and still is, a process. We often come upon hindrances in our journey, and then we must come through them, and the Word helps us to do that.

THE BIBLE IS GREAT

I must say the Bible is great. Did I think so at first? No! I thought it was interesting, and if you like history, it's loaded with it. There's story after story and event after event. But the Bible has come to mean so much more to me.

Life with God is such a wonder! Every day He has something new to say, or reveal, to me, and He'll do the same for you, if you want Him to. I'm nothing special, and God wants all men and women everywhere to know Him as heavenly Father, Abba, and also to know His Son, Jesus Christ.

God's will is that we all grow in the faith and knowledge of this, His Son, Jesus, and, although this is not a difficult process, it does take time. Knowing Him comes through His Word, the Bible, and by His Spirit. After having experienced this now for many years, I have to say that it has been worth it all. God can teach anyone, and it's not dependent upon your IQ. No, all that is needed is a willing heart and some patience on your part. For me, it has required a good dictionary too.

PROVERBS IS FILLED WITH
WISDOM AND INSTRUCTION

As I noted in an earlier chapter, Proverbs is a good example of a book that is filled with wisdom and instruction. In fact, within its thirty-one chapters, it has wisdom galore and instruction "all over the place." Proverbs, for example, clearly teaches us consequences. If you do this, then this or that will happen.

The fact that God speaks of consequences is for the good of us all. He doesn't want you or me to be in error, to be misled or, worse yet, to be fools. He doesn't want us to have to go through unnecessary events or incur unnecessary problems. If we know His wisdom and seek His understanding and His instruction, and we pay attention, or give heed, to it, then we can miss, or sidestep, such troubles.

Proverbs tells us so much about God's Spirit, that it is the Spirit of Wisdom, and that this wisdom calls us to come to Him and to know and receive from Him as well. This book offers to all mankind what we don't even know we need and can have: wisdom, knowledge, understanding and good judgment.

God uses His Holy Spirit to impart all of this to us through His Word. All we need to do is pay attention and respond when He calls to us. How do we do that? Just by giving ear and paying heed to what the Spirit of God speaks. If you don't want to do that, of course, you can go your own way, but you will surely end up not liking what you have chosen for yourself.

A POWERFUL CHAPTER

Proverbs 1 is a powerful chapter, and you might want to take time to read it all and then stop and think about what is being said. Better yet, read it out loud and slowly, stopping when you begin to hear what God is saying to you personally. He speaks through His words that are recorded in the Bible.

In addition, as noted previously, you can ask God for His thoughts on any matter. He does have them, and they're good. They may not be what you want to hear at the moment, and you may not agree with them, but ask anyway. You'll see that His thoughts are worthwhile and really good.

I ask God for His thoughts because His thoughts are higher then mine, as are His ways (see Isaiah 55:8-9). He likes us to come upward. Do not most fathers and mothers want more for their children? He is so pleased by this that He proves it to us. We just need to be aware of His presence with us and of His hand that is working in our lives.

You can choose to take a journey with God, and in the process, you will come to know Him better. You will come to know and receive His love, for, as we have noted, He is love.

God does this all by the Holy Spirit. He is the one who brings love to you by shedding abroad the love of God in your heart (see Romans 5:5). He can do it, and He's ready to do it, so it depends upon you. Believe me, you really should want God's great love.

I'm smiling as I write this to you because it's so powerful. If you would like to stop right here for a while and just talk things over with God, please do. Recognize Him as the Father, who is love, and let Him and His love come to you. If you have hate in your heart, or whatever, even if you're somehow at odds with God, talk it over with

Him, let Him drive all of that hate out, and let His love cover it.

ARE WE TO BE DOORMATS?

If you want to know what God, who is love, looks like or acts like, or what His faith in action is all about, open your New Testament and begin to read at Matthew, the first book, and continue through Revelation, the last book. The Old Testament is very "cool" too. There's a lot there to digest, but it's all good.

Does this mean that now you'll be a doormat for others, or that nothing will ever bother you? No, but with God and His love in you, you'll no longer want to lash out at others. Love doesn't do that. I can say this because one day, many years ago, I learned what loves does and does not do.

THIS IS NOT LOVE!

I was about to use a belt to punish my then-young son, and as I was about to do it, a God thought suddenly came to my mind (I now know this only in hindsight). The thought was: This is not love. I immediately stopped what I was doing, giving heed to the voice within, and I never used a belt again.

Sometime later I came to know exactly what to do. I started seeking God for more wisdom regarding what to do and how to do it, as well, since what I knew and did as a mom was not working. I discovered Proverbs in the Bible to be a great parenting book. That was God's source for the wisdom I was asking Him for. In it, I learned that discipline and punishment were two very different things.

Discipline, I learned, is a training, something we teach, demonstrate and do with and for our children, and it's crucial that they learn obedience. But does this require that we be mean or act like a dictator? No! Not at all! Children need boundaries (although not to the extreme), and they even like having them (although you wouldn't think so if you heard their complaining).

Instead of that belt, I began using a red paddle, and I explained to each of my children when and why I would use it. I told them that the paddle would only be used if they disobeyed, and that was all it was to be used for. I would never threaten to use it, but once I took it in hand, I *would* use it.

It worked, and this eliminated many of my wrong actions, taken out of pent-up emotions. After a while, that red paddle was rarely used. It just hung there beside a pancake turner next to our stovetop. That was a great victory for all of us, for it paved the way for more peace and self-control in our home.

> *I started seeking God for more wisdom regarding what to do and how to do it as well!*

CHILDREN SOMETIMES NEED US TO BE THE "BAD GUY"

Children sometimes need Mom or Dad to be the "bad guy" so that they can "save face" with their friends. When a parent says, "No, you can't go," it often helps the child out of a difficult situation. I overheard one of my children talking on the phone one day with a friend, saying, "My mom says I can't go." Then looked relieved as they hung up the phone. There are times when your child, especially a teenager, may be secretly glad that you said no. It gives them an "easy out" so they don't have to go.

Even babies need your firm no. Despite their cute and oh-so-disarming ways, they also need to be taught. Children of all ages seem to know what buttons to push to take advantage of their parents. This shows an amazing talent on their part to study you, know your weaknesses and then work you over when you least expect it.

Children do this to you moms when you're on the phone, when you're in a store, right before bedtime or when you're tired and/or busy, so you won't necessarily be able to think through their "con."

It seems to me that this ability comes to children somewhere between the time they begin to walk and the time they become potty trained.

They are very smart, for they would never dare do this to their dad. Why not? They know instinctively not to arouse a sleeping giant.

FATHERS HAVE AN IMPORTANT ROLE TO PLAY

I must say what some might not want to hear, and that is: I believe that the husband and father of the family is endowed with wisdom from God that the wife doesn't always have. It was no accident that God created both male and female. The two balance each other.

Men and women are so different, and rightly so, as each brings something to the family that is sorely needed. When one or the other is missing from the home for any reason, it represents a great loss for the children. God created both man and woman, and He had a reason for doing it. In our society of broken homes, this is a tough thing to hear, but it's the truth anyway.

Some men tend to avoid confrontation when at all possible, but when it does become necessary, they know how to deal with it, although families suffer terribly when a father or a mother is overbearing, demanding or abusive in word and/or action.

Just because a parent lets a child have his way doesn't mean that it was right and good for them. A parent may let something go because they're unable to deal with it at the moment, but it usually means that the child is missing out on God's best for them. Please do think about this, even though you may not want to.

BOB KNEW WHAT WAS RIGHT

Why do I share this here? Through hindsight, I have come to know the great importance of it. My husband

133

Bob knew what was right, and he, too, loved his family, but he didn't always say what he thought. He preferred to hold his peace.

His "no" was sure and unchangeable, not at all wishy-washy, as mine could be. It was that peace and quiet assurance of his, plus a certain West Virginia charm, that drew me. As you might have guessed, he's with the Lord now. We had forty years of marriage together. I miss his arms around me in the night, and his quiet prayers to God on my behalf.

> *We had forty years of marriage together!*

At various times, he would say to me that he wasn't sleeping; he was praying for his family and others. Was Bob perfect? No, but then neither was I. We had our differences to be sure, and this fact forced me to seek God for answers, solutions and help.

At times, God would lead me to fast and pray. This would usually be for a leader or some happening going on in which God wanted His outcome or will to prevail. I only did this by His leading, never on my own. Why? Because it was a spiritual battle. What caused me to say yes to the Lord's request, would I fast, was that the battle was His and not mine (see 2 Chronicles 20:15), plus knowing that Jesus always finishes what He starts would cause me to become glad, for God and His good outcome. I never prayed from my opinion, only by God's leading and what scriptures He caused me to know and decree.

ENJOY YOUR SPOUSE NOW

There is something I must share here that I learned soon after Bob had left this world. I believed that it was his time to go, but I missed him terribly. Love your spouse and enjoy your time with them while you can. Nothing else is more important. I now realize that I said no to Bob far too many times, and I allowed our house and my own interests to take priority over what he wanted to do.

So what if what your spouse likes is not what you like and seems boring to you? I've learned that what really matters is being with them and loving them. And you can ask God to help you to connect in the way you should and to come to find enjoyment in each other's activities. Sadly, I never thought to pray this prayer until just now.

We always tend to think that because a person is seemingly healthy we have all the time in the world together, and yet the call to leave this world can be just a breath away—for any of us.

It wasn't that I didn't love my husband. I surely did. But after he was gone, I realized that I could have loved him in action a whole lot more.

BACK TO PROVERBS

Well, now, let's get back to Proverbs. I would encourage you to examine this wonderful book for yourself. Keep a Bible in your bathroom for those sit-down times. I have one in mine.

For me, the changes from having my mind renewed by talking to God and hearing His voice, not just reading His Word, the Bible, came gradually, one step at a time. Often, when I was in church, hearing the pastor's message, I would silently pray, "Okay, God. Now how do I do this?" I knew it wasn't enough just to hear and agree. I needed to put the new teaching into action.

Many years before, the Lord, by His Spirit, had corrected me one day. I had just finished changing a diaper on my toddler and set him loose again when a God-thought came to me. It was this: "You're hearing all the teachings, but you're not yet a doer."

Immediately I looked up and said, "I'm sorry, God. Help me to be a doer too, and not just a hearer only." Well, needless to say, He has been helping me ever since.

HEAVEN, OUR GOAL

Do I deserve His help? No, but He and I both know I need it "big time." I needed it then, and I still need it. I won't arrive until this journey is over and I get there, "there" being Heaven. God has said:

And hath raised us up together, and made us sit together in heavenly places in Christ Jesus.

Ephesians 2:6

This passage refers to the here and now, but I believe it also refers to the future.

GROWING PAINS

God loves us and is not out to hurt anyone, only to encourage us to grow, to grow up, to grow in grace and in the knowledge of our Lord and Savior, Jesus Christ. So there is a real faith to be had and actions that must accompany it.

I wasn't so much wrong in my faith. No! Not at all! I just had too little of it. The faith I had in Jesus was that He was born (and so we celebrate Christmas), and He died (and so we celebrate Easter). On these two occasions, my focus was mostly on presents, shopping and holiday meals. I have to say, though, that the Christmas Eve service was always special to me, and when we got home, there was a certain, wonderful, peace in our home. As we sat on the couch and chairs watching television, I would be silently counting all the children and, in my heart, being very thankful to God for all of them.

CHILDREN ARE A GIFT FROM GOD

It was (and still is) a wonder to me that God would allow me to have these children, for although I loved and wanted children, I was lacking on many fronts and surely unqualified for the job. Thankfully, God gave us seven great gifts, and there is not one of them that I could do without.

Truly children are a gift from God. I didn't always know it, but I know it now. Through my children, I was forced to become patient and to grow and mature in many ways—especially with God. Why with God? Because although I knew I needed counseling, I reasoned that doing it would take food off of our table. Besides, God could counsel me, and His counsel wouldn't cost a dime. I'm so glad that I got His kind of counsel and help. There's nothing in this world that can compare to it.

LEARNING THAT GOD WAS MY HELP

I must say that many years ago something major happened to cause me to be able to receive God's counsel. There was short-term help from two people, but that ended when one moved away and the other said, "I can't help you anymore." More time went on, and I muddled through, until a day when I realized fully that I needed big-time help. But what was I to do? There was no one.

I stood there, thinking and searching for what could help me. Here's what I thought: "I can't go talk to people, for they will gossip. I can't call home, for I would be told, 'You made your bed; now lie in it.' I can't do drugs, for that will fry your brain. I can't do suicide, for that would be a one-way ticket to Hell." I walked over to the bedroom window and, while looking at the sunset, said, "God, if You don't help me, I don't know what I'm going to do." I stood there as the colors in the sky blended into night, and then I quietly left the room. I really can't pinpoint what God did, but somehow, little by little, I was suddenly getting help. God became my Helper.

In case you're wondering why I didn't go to my husband, the few times I did, he would say, "What do you want me to do?" Plus, he was hardworking and worked long hours. I would look at him when he came home and think, "How can I 'unload' on him?" I just couldn't do that to him. He was already so tired.

Surely I can say, *"My help cometh from the LORD, which made heaven and earth"* (Psalm 121:2). And *"for he shall deliver the needy when he crieth; the poor also, and him that hath no helper"* (Psalm 72:12).

How about you? If you like, God can be your Helper as well. He is no respecter of persons. Look up different scriptures on *help* and *helper*. They can, indeed, increase your faith. It's not instant, as the results of some of the harmful choices we make, but the

> *Truly children are a gift from God! I didn't always know it, but I know it now!*

peace of mind He can give you is worth waiting for, as is His wisdom and counsel that comes either directly, by sudden insight or through gleaning His good Word.

This took much time, effort, prayer and God's grace

(along with the rather constant use of a dictionary) to glean from His wonderful and good Word. I must also note the many times, throughout the years, when I and others went forward for prayer in response to our pastor's invitation. When this happened, others, who were not in the need of prayer at that moment, would come and stand behind us and help pray for us. Their prayers made a great difference in my life.

Your prayers are also powerful because when you pray, you're inviting God into your situation or circumstances, and when you don't want to do that, He is left on the outside, wanting to come in, but unable to do so. Seeking God is the pathway to blessing.

BACK TO CHRISTMAS AND EASTER

Well, as you noticed, I got sidetracked again, so now let's get back to what I was saying. Again I encourage you to read what we call the gospels—the books of Matthew, Mark, Luke and John. In these books, you will find all that went on before and after Christmas and through Easter, including Jesus appearing to so many after His resurrection. In these books, many important truths concerning who He is are very clearly recorded. As you will see, there was a whole lot going on then.

And it's still continuing today. If you want to see how, then go on to read the book of Acts that follows the gospel books. Then, as you are able, there are the letters, or epistles, to the churches written primarily by Saint Paul, Saint Peter and Saint John, and, finally, the book of Revelation.

This may sound like a lot, but it really isn't. Why not get started today? The journey will be well worth your while.

THE COST

Will it cost you something? Yes and no. Yes, it will require time and energy, but no, you don't have to pay the price. Jesus Christ already did that with His body. He shed His blood for you and me.

The pretty crosses we see in churches can do little to move us. They didn't move me until I read in the Bible a description of what happened to the body of Jesus when He was killed—those thirty-nine stripes, that is, one lashing and gouging after another, and each one pulling and yanking at His body. Just think, this was done to Jesus thirty-nine times. Oh, the pain, the blood, and His body so marred that He no longer looked human. Seeing a cross showing Jesus with a spot of blood on Him so misrepresents the true reality about His shed blood.

The meaning and value of His shed blood is not always fully known or understood these days, although the men and women in the late 1800s and early 1900s surely did understand it, or those songs could not have been composed. I have five old hymnals from that time period, and they contain songs about the blood of Christ and what it did for us on the cross of Calvary. They knew that these songs and their truths moved people's hearts when they sang them or heard them sung. The reality affected them so that they could not help but turn to God in tears and repentance.

THAT THOUGHT "GOT TO ME"

"You have to learn to keep yourself, to keep yourself from iniquity! ... Like a weed, sin will try to come back and take control of you!"

We're all sinners, and, for me, it took a long time to reconcile myself to this truth. In fact, it took me one whole year. I remember our priest reading from the book of John during a Bible study and saying that we were all sinners. Well those words "got to me." God was saying that I was a sinner, yet I thought, "I don't feel like it or know it, but still God said it. And how come I didn't know it?" Well, like I said, it took me a long time to come to terms with what I never really heard or knew before.

I can't say it wasn't taught. Maybe it was, and I just didn't "get it" or didn't make the connection. How about you? Are there truths about God you didn't get either or make the connection?

But when I did "get it," this truth certainly moved me along in my journey with God. I "got it" one day, by the help of God's Spirit, for I just suddenly knew. I just knew I was indeed a sinner, and so I was finally able to reconcile this truth to myself.

THIS REVELATION FREED ME

What was really "neat" about this experience was this: when I finally recognized that I was a sinner, then I knew that I was no longer a sinner. Realizing what I was had freed me to become what I was destined to be. I am so glad that I didn't let go or quit trying to understand this truth. Why it took me so long to come to this, I'm not sure. Maybe it was because we are led to believe, by some, that it's our being "good" that will get us to Heaven. Please know that this is not the case at all. No, we are only assured of Heaven because of Jesus' life and because He took upon Himself the sins of all mankind, shedding His precious blood to cover those sins. In the process, He had to die, but then came the resurrection. It was the perfect sacrifice and actions of Jesus on the cross that paid our entrance fee into Heaven—nothing that we could have done.

BE PATIENT WITH GOD

So, please hold steady with the things of God, and when you don't understand something, or you don't like something, be patient with Him and with what He does and doesn't do for you, or for someone you're praying for. God is never too slow, and it's never the case that He doesn't hear or doesn't care. There is usually a lot that you and I don't know or understand. To charge or blame God is a foolish act, for if you do that, you are really cutting yourself off from the Source of all life.

So dig in, stay put and stay faithful to God, whether

your journey is just beginning or in the middle or already close to the end. Faith in God is where the action is, so maintain your faith.

God had faith in His Son, Jesus, He has faith in you and He is looking for faith on your part. Faith is what moves Him, and unbelief is what holds Him back. It was said of Jesus:

> *And He did not many mighty works there because of their unbelief.* Matthew 13:58

Get into the Bible so that your faith can grow. Paul declared to the Roman believers:

> *So then faith cometh by hearing and hearing by the word of God.* Romans 10:17

AN INSPIRED WORD

Our life is like a garden, and it's up to us to tend it. There are the seeds and the plants they produce, and then there are the weeds. You need to tend to them both, and this is an effort, to be sure. But the rewards are surer yet.

Allow me to share an inspired word that came to me by the Holy Spirit one morning after I had finished spending time with God in the Psalms. He said: "You have to learn to keep yourself, to keep yourself from iniquity. Although you've made your confession and, indeed, your heart is right, still, like a weed, sin will try to come back and take control of you, thus stopping you in your tracks. Learn to pray it away, even as you would chop a weed out. Sing My songs of deliverance, and the enemy will be held at bay."

It's not that I'm such a good gardener (as the small plot in my backyard reveals), but with God's help, I will continue to personally grow in faith and action.

How about you? Do you sense God is reaching out to you? Or maybe He's been doing it for a while now. Could this be the time to respond and extend your arms back to Him?

God, our heavenly Father, does not mean for us to have only religion (although maybe our faith has its beginnings there). His will is for us to be in relationship with Him, and such a relationship can only come through His Son, Jesus. There is no other way, and if you doubt that, you'd better reconsider, for even the devil himself recognizes and believes that Jesus is God's only begotten Son.

DON'T WAIT

Really, you don't have to wait until you get to Heaven to have a personal relationship with God and His Son. If that were not true, why would Jesus have told us to pray to the Father? And why would the Father have taught us to pray using Jesus' name. It all sounds very personal to me. What do you think?

Will you have some ups and downs in this relationship? Probably. But this won't be God's fault or His mistake. So, just stay steady, even when you're tired or get "bothered" in some way. Don't fall for Satan's very subtle temptations to quit on God or the faith you've been given. When you cast your faith away, your life becomes shipwrecked. Here's what God has to say about that:

> *Holding faith, and a good conscience; which some having put away concerning faith have made shipwreck.*
> 1 Timothy 1:19

So, dear reader, why not consider making your confession of faith? Then, take your stand and keep your faith in action. Stay active in faith, in hope and in love, and you won't ever be sorry you did. ❦

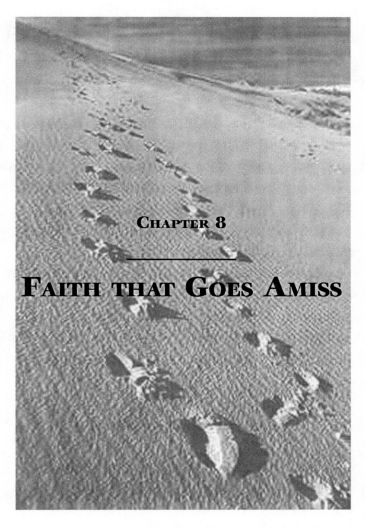

CHAPTER 8

FAITH THAT GOES AMISS

Beware lest any man spoil you through philosophy and vain deceit, after the tradition of men, after the rudiments of the world, and not after Christ. For in him dwelleth all the fulness of the Godhead bodily.

Colossians 2:8-9

"It's not your fault, God, that I am what I am. I can't go

with the thought I just had: You knew when You chose me what I was. No, that would be a deflection of my failure onto You. I'm destined to get better, and You're the one who enables me to do it.

"I need your help to fill in the gaps. You've already been the bridge for my times of unbelief, and now You must have a word for these gaps, shortcomings, even failures. You supply all my needs according to Your riches in glory by Christ Jesus (see Philippians 4:19). So, Abba, I'm looking to You and to Your Son, Jesus, the Author and Finisher of my faith (see Hebrews 12:2).

"I need your help, Dear Helper. I still need more growing and more renewing of the mind. It's a good thing that You, O most High, are so capable! You're able to do exceedingly, abundantly more than I can think or ask according to the power that works in me (see Ephesians 3:20)."

What's This All About?

Now you may be wondering what this is all about. Well, these were my thoughts to God this very morning. I sensed that I had missed it with Him the evening before while spending time with a friend. God has a way of letting you know where you stand with Him. Of course, I felt bad, but I wasn't sure where exactly I had "blown it."

I mentally searched for my point of failure, and eventually pinpointed two moments, one in which I failed to speak up as I should have and another when I reasoned my thoughts away. Because of this, I did not fully share as I might have, and since things were still not right within me, this is how I came before the Lord this morning. Something was still amiss; something was not quite right somewhere.

I almost put my missing it on God, by saying to Him, "Well, You chose me." I might as well have said, "What do You expect?"

GOD WANTS US IN HIS FAMILY

God wants us in His family, but it's not automatic in any sense of the word. The growing I've been talking about, the daily receiving of grace and help from Him, and then the ability to serve Him and do some good work that He enables and anoints us for all require something of us and our faith in God.

God has a way of letting you know where you stand with Him!

The problem is that we can sometimes go amiss in our faith, when we measure God against what we think we know or by our own opinion or the opinion of others. He can only be measured by His Word, and to do that we must compare scripture to scripture.

Without meaning to do it, we sometimes bring God down to our level, and this causes our faith to go amiss. There is faith present, but it's a little "messed up." Without meaning to do it, we sometimes view God as small or too busy to help us. We may think that our little "stuff" doesn't matter to Him or that He's way out there somewhere, too far to reach at the moment. If that's the case with you, then I have some good news. Absolutely everything about you does matter to this great and mighty God and Father. He just needs us to have faith in Him.

GOD WORKS IN THE REALM OF FAITH

God works in the realm of faith, and the adversary to your life and mine works in the realm of fear and doubt. Therefore, God wants us to be in faith and belief, and Satan wants us to fear and doubt (which is the absence of faith) and not believe God. Somehow it actually seems easier to be in fear and doubt than it is to walk in faith, and some of this is because of the world's way and influence on us. What's really amiss is that we're thinking small and have small thoughts about God, and so our faith has become limp.

We sometimes mistake hope for faith. We're always hoping for this or that, hoping that God will do something or other for us, when, in truth, His Word has already stated very clearly what He will do and even what our part in that action must be. So we could know what we have to do to make it happen. This is the reason I included, at the beginning of this chapter, my very personal time with God and the thoughts and prayers I exchanged with Him today.

TIME WITH GOD

There was a time in my life when I was very inconsistent in my relationship with God. For example, I didn't have fellowship with Him every single morning. I would sense Him drawing me, but because of something I wanted to do, I would put Him off. I was busy with other things perhaps, or I just wanted to finish watching some TV show. Then God got my attention one day while I was reading the book of Esther.

Esther lived in Old Testament times and was the queen chosen for King Ahasuerus of Persia. There had been another queen before her, a woman named Vashti. Vashti was a very beautiful woman, and the king was proud to have her as his queen, but when he wanted her to come to one of his banquets so that he could show her off to the people, she refused to go. As a result, she was deposed, and Esther was chosen to replace her.

When I read that, it quickly dawned on me that I was doing this same thing to God. I was refusing to come when the King beckoned, and this was not just any king. This was the King of kings and Lord of lords. I quickly did some confessing and repenting, for I surely did not want to be banished from His presence and never be called again. Would God do such a thing? I don't know, but I'm not about to test Him on it.

Can you see how God uses the experiences of others, even from ancient times, to teach us? We surely all need both the Old and the New Testaments of the Bible. Why? Because God is in all of it!

How about you? Have you been inconsistent or half-hearted with God? Have you even refused Him or resisted Him? Please stop and think about this. Pray about it, and then come back to the book, for I'm about to shift gears, so to speak.

SOMETHING ELSE THAT'S AMISS

> *Jesus offers you grace and truth, and the devil offers you lies and temptations!*

There is something else that may be amiss or missing in your faith. The Bible addresses it in what God said through Saint Paul:

Neither give place to the devil.
Ephesians 4:27

Many give him place and don't even realize it. All of us have to face temptation. Did he not present Jesus Himself with three powerful temptations? And what did Jesus do? He responded, but not out of His own reasoning. Instead, He used the sacred Scriptures, the Word of God, to do battle with the enemy.

What does that tell you? I know what it told me. If the very King of Glory needed to use scripture against the devil and his temptations, how could I do anything less? Sure, it takes an effort for us to know the Scriptures, but why would we ever go into battle with little or no ammunition to use against such a powerful foe? He has plenty of ammunition to use against us. Of this you can be sure.

Are we still being tempted as Jesus was? You'd better know and believe we are. Temptation comes to us in many forms, but since the enemy knows our personal weaknesses, the temptations sent our way are often tailor-made for us. No wonder God has declared:

> *Watch and pray, that ye enter not into temptation: the spirit indeed is willing, but the flesh is weak.*
>
> Matthew 26:41

Jesus Himself taught us to pray, *"Our Father, ... lead us not into temptation, but deliver us from evil"* (Matthew 6:9 and 13). I encourage you to pray this for yourself and your entire family. It's not that we must focus on evil, but we must not be ignorant or unaware of it either.

Two Camps

There are two camps in the world. One is God's camp. He created this world, and His Son, Jesus, will come back again to rule it. The other camp is Satan's. He is called *"the god of this world"* (2 Corinthians 4:4). He will one day be cast into what is called *"the lake of fire"* with all those who chose to follow him (Revelation 19:20 and 20:10).

Jesus offers you grace and truth, and the devil offers you lies and temptations. And guess what? You get to choose between the two. Depending on your choice, your life could be either awesome or awful.

Christ, the Author and Finisher of our faith, offers no temptation, just the real goods—life here and now on earth and life eternal with Him in Heaven.

Jesus also offers you a lifetime of help. He is the great Helper. He offers you His grace, His wisdom, His knowledge, His understanding, His counsel and His teachings—sound doctrine.

THE THRONE OF GRACE

The Lord also offers you a place to come to called *"the throne of grace."* It is described in the book of Hebrews:

Seeing then that we have a great high priest, that is passed into the heavens, Jesus the Son of God, let us hold fast our profession. For we have not an high priest which cannot be touched with the feeling of our infirmities; but was in all points tempted like as we are, yet without sin. Let us therefore come boldly unto the throne of grace, that we may obtain mercy, and find grace to help in time of need. Hebrews 4:14-16

What do you think? Does this sound like a place you would like to go to?

Would you like for Jesus, the great High Priest, to bring you to the truth, His Word, and then to love you and restore your soul?

And please don't forget all of His benefits. Some of them are found in the beautiful Psalm 103:

Bless the LORD, O my soul, and forget not all his benefits:

Who forgiveth all thine iniquities; who healeth all thy diseases;

Who redeemeth thy life from destruction; who crowneth thee with lovingkindness and tender mercies;

Who satisfieth thy mouth with good things; so that thy youth is renewed like the eagle's. Psalm 103:2-5

Forgiveness of all your iniquities, healing for all your diseases, the redemption of your life from destruction, your crowning with lovingkindness and tender mercies, the satisfaction of your mouth with good things and the renewing of your youth. Wow! That sounds like great benefits to me. What do you think?

There are many blessings to be had, but there are also many curses (see Deuteronomy 28). The choice is ours.

WHAT CAN THE GOD OF THIS WORLD OFFER US?

What can the god of this world offer us? For starters, he has counterfeits and deceptions, and then he has tricks, half-truths and outright lies. I'm sad to say that I've fallen for some of these, placed very subtly in my way. It gives me no joy to tell it, but if it can help someone else to avoid them, then I'm happy.

Knowing the truth will set you free. Of course, in the end, it's up to you to make the right choice, to believe what God says and to act upon it.

Remember, the devil, the adversary of your soul, your

body and your spirit (and you're all of this), always comes to cast doubt and fear. Those are his major identifying signs (and they are major). He tries to bring fear, not only to individuals, but also to the masses. He speaks through many sources, and his lies are numerous.

As a side note: doesn't it seem odd that terrible events happen at about the same time in different places, and this inflames public fear, and the result is that new laws are passed further restricting our freedoms? Doesn't it somehow make you wonder who or what is behind it all?

Putting Faith in Something or Someone Other than God

Recently I learned firsthand about the real source for our protection. As I was locking my back door at bedtime one evening, God, by His Spirit, revealed to me that it wasn't the locked door that was protecting me; it was He. In that moment, my faith in God, in His care and in His protection, greatly increased.

Of course, that doesn't mean that I should stop locking my door. He was just letting me know that I had misplaced my faith. That faith was amiss. Rather than being in the lock, however good that lock happened to be, it needed to be in Him alone.

Predicting Negative Events

What about the faith that is amiss in those who go about predicting this and that negative event, as if on a bandwagon. Then others hop on so that eventually it comes to pass. How? By their faith in it. Without knowing, people call it in, instead of using faith in God to tell it to cease. Thus, the masses are being used as pawns to promote destruction and more fear.

Oh, how the adversary, the devil, must laugh and enjoy what he sees going on here in this country! His tactics seem to be working, even when most people say they don't believe that he even exists. Far too many don't know how to put him under their feet. I wouldn't know it either, had not God revealed it to me through His Word and His sent Helper, the Holy Spirit.

BEING EMPOWERED BY THE HOLY SPIRIT

Again, He is greatly needed in your life and in your journey to and with God. Just as Jesus needed to be empowered and filled with the Holy Spirit, so do we. We all need to follow His leading, and we all need the gifts that He alone gives.

As I was locking my back door at bedtime one evening, God, by His Spirit, revealed to me that it wasn't the locked door that was protecting me; it was He!

157

These gifts are for the building up of the Church, the Body of Christ. If you don't believe this, then your faith is certainly amiss, and I would certainly be amiss not to share this with you. Take it to heart, for it is crucial, not only to have and believe Jesus and His Word, but also to have and believe in His Spirit and His functions in the world as well.

TRUE SALVATION

It is not enough to have what I call an intellectual salvation. Those who have it mentally assent to receiving salvation, but they have no true heart conversion. You must acknowledge Jesus as God's only Son, and you must also acknowledge your sins, confessing them to God right then and there, and forsaking them. This is necessary; otherwise you have a "cheap salvation."

True salvation came with a terrible price. God risked everything, putting His own beloved Son at risk of facing a devil's Hell. But Jesus overcame every temptation known to man, and He used the Word of God to do it. His entire journey on this earth was for you and me.

Never take this lightly or join in with those who joke and jeer about it, and so become a mouthpiece for Satan. We must not only have faith in Jesus, but also faith in His shed blood. Why? Because, as we have noted, without the shedding of His blood there would have been no remission for any and all of the sins of mankind (see Hebrews 9:22).

THE IMPORTANCE OF THE COMMUNION

Is it any wonder, then, that God, our heavenly Father, wants us to take communion in our services? We do this *"in remembrance"* of the sacrifice of His Son, Jesus (1 Corinthians 11:24-25). His body was broken for our healing, and His blood was shed for our sins. I know I don't understand it all, and I already have touched on this, but there is more.

I recall reading early on, in the book of Genesis (the very first book in the Bible), about the two sons of Adam and Eve (Cain and Abel), how Cain rose up against his brother Abel and killed him. When God asked him where his brother was, Cain answered that he didn't know, saying *"Am I my brother's keeper?"* (Genesis 4:9).

And, secondly, about the voice of his brother's blood that cried out from the ground to God:

And he said, What hast thou done? the voice of thy brother's blood crieth unto me from the ground.
Genesis 4:10

Well, in reading that account, it caused me to think about the blood of Christ Jesus. Does the blood of Jesus speak too? If so (and I believe it does), then His shed blood must be more meaningful then I know or ever thought. Surely it was and is to God!

If the blood of Abel was speaking, then surely the blood of Jesus must be speaking too. Please do not discount any of the truths regarding Jesus and His blood. There is life in that blood for you today.

If Jesus had not poured out His blood for us, then the salvation of man from his sins would be impossible. These old hymns about the blood of Jesus still need to be sung. When they are removed as "no longer relevant" or "offensive to many people," then the devil is gleeful. Why? Then he doesn't have to be constantly reminded of the fact that Jesus defeated him ever so "royally" on the cross and took back from him the power and authority he had so deceptively stolen from the first Adam.

If Jesus had not poured out His blood for us, then the salvation of man from his sins would be impossible!

PRINCE OF THE POWER OF THE AIR

In case you're unaware of it, your adversary is also known as *"the prince of the power of the air, the spirit that now worketh in the children of disobedience"* (Ephesians 2:2). Could it be possible that doing things contrary to God's will (disobedience) affects more of us then we know?

As I noted once before, there were times when God,

by His Spirit, would lead me with the question: "Would you renounce Satan and all his works?" Very quickly, I would answer, "Oh, yes, God! I don't want to touch him 'with a ten-foot pole'!" Then I would say out loud, "I do renounce Satan and all his works." And that would be that.

This exercise, however, would always cause me to think. What had I exposed myself to or what had I done without consciously knowing it? So, whenever you sense that God is leading you to renounce Satan and his works, don't fuss about the details or even be "put off," or offended by the question. Just verbally do so. What do you have to lose?

THE IMPORTANT QUESTION

In my early years, this question, "Do you renounce Satan and all his works?" was always asked in the Catholic ceremony of christening for babies. The priest would ask the question, and then those present would respond, out loud, "Yes, I do." I've noticed, however, in the last few baptismal ceremonies I attended, that the question was no longer being asked. I found this to be very sad. When that questions was asked, it was a wonderful opportunity for people to renounce Satan and all his works, which they, most likely, didn't even know they were a part of. Now that opportunity was gone. The need to renounce Satan and his works is not being taught nearly enough.

Please know that one of the stated reasons that Jesus Christ, the Son of God, came to this earth was to *"destroy the works of the devil"* (1 John 3:8). So when you renounce him, you're doing what Jesus did.

Our words and our confession matter, even though they may sometimes seem only ceremonial and not real substance. God knows the difference, and it's no accident that this truth is being presented to you. It may make you a bit uncomfortable, but it could also be a key that unlocks an important door for you or releases you out of some known or unknown snare set just for you.

Being Set Free from Bondages Brought About by Fear

So now, let's get back to where I was going. Fear and doubt are "biggies," but you can be set free from any bondage they bring you into. This will be done for you, as it was for me, by God's Word, which *"is truth"* (John 17:17), and by His Spirit.

Many times, God has revealed to me the painful truth about some situation of my life. I say "painful" because He showed me that the situation was the result of some sin or wrongdoing on my part. Was that a pleasurable experience? No, not at all! Seeing the truth about ourselves can be very painful, but it can also set us free. So let God have His way with you.

It "Smarts"

I don't need to tell you that it can "smart" when someone says something that hurts your feelings. One day someone let loose a "zinger" that hit me hard. This person seemed oblivious to the fact that what they had said hurt me so deeply, but it caused me to search my soul. Was there some truth to what had been said?

I ask myself this question often in such situations, and I find that sometimes there is some truth behind the comments, and sometimes there isn't. How can I know? Because God knows, and I ask Him to reveal it to me. The revelation doesn't always come instantly, but as I come before Him, He speaks to me through His written Word, the Bible.

In case this might seem discouraging to some, please don't allow it to be. Long ago, I discovered the fact, through the book of James, that if I am willing to confess my sins, I can be healed (again, see James 5:16). At the time, I needed a lot of healing, and if that was the way to get it, then it was okay with me. So I would humble myself and admit before God what I was and what I wasn't, and He healed me.

I should tell you that I didn't do this dry-eyed. Repentance is usually accompanied by tears, and if tears come to you, please don't hold them back. They are an important part of the cleansing process.

You Don't Have to Beg God for Forgiveness

I have never had to beg God for forgiveness. He said:
The blood of Jesus Christ his Son cleanseth us from all sin.
If we confess our sins, he is faithful and just to forgive us our sins, and to cleanse us from all unrighteousness.
1 John 1:7 and 9

Every sin I can discover in myself and confess and forsake is one less sin that I will be judged for one day. I don't know about you, but I want to have my slate as clean as possible. At first, it seems very difficult to eat humble pie, but after a while, it gets easier. I think I've had more than my share.

In the moment that God reveals any sin in your life, think of yourself as being at a major intersection. You can either choose to continue as you are, or you can take a new turn in your life, one that will lead you to something new and far better.

I've had many such intersections in life. At the time, it feels a little like we've come to a stop sign, but, in reality, it's God's intervention on our behalf. It may be coming to you because of the prayers of someone else. It may be coming from a person who tries to talk to you about God, and you think you can't stand them or the things they say. Wherever it comes from, you can be sure that it's all happening because of God's love for you.

The divine interventions or intersections we encounter in life usually seem like needless interruptions. But, be careful! This could be a beginning point for your journey, your journey to God and to love.

So, it's time to wake up. Let your eyes be opened, and your heart and soul as well, because Jesus, the King, is coming. Believe me, when He comes, you don't want to have your faith about Him, His Word or His sent Holy Spirit to be amiss.

I know I may be giving you a lot, but you need to hear and come to know for yourself all that God has inspired me to share in these pages.

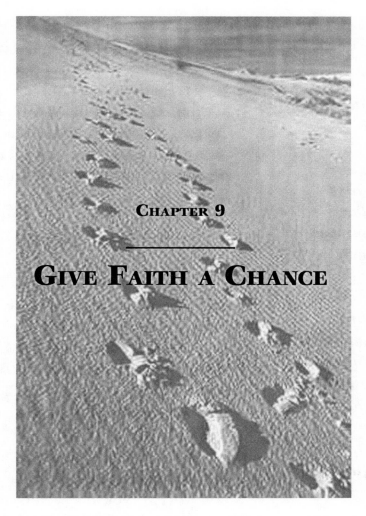

CHAPTER 9

GIVE FAITH A CHANCE

*I can do all things through Christ which strengtheneth
me.* Philippians 4:13

"Yes, give faith a chance, although you probably
have." Just recently that was the thought God inspired
me with. We must never let go or drift away from what
we have heard and believed from Him. We must not al-

low others, or even ourselves, to cast doubt upon it. If we allow this to happen, our faith becomes like a fire that is slowly being smothered and put out.

Rather than allow the fire of our faith to grow cold and die, we must do all that we can to get that blaze going and then keep it going.

IT'S YOUR FAITH

Just know, it's your faith that moved you into action, and whether others cheer you on or just stare in disbelief, it doesn't matter!

Just know, it's your faith that moved you into action, and whether others cheer you on or just stare in disbelief, it doesn't matter. Don't let the reaction of others bother you. It's your life in Christ that's at stake. Besides, it's your faith, not theirs.

Be happy when you're in faith because that's a very good place to be. At first, you may have some uncertainties: Did I really hear from God? Or is this just my own thinking? Ask Him about it, and He'll confirm it to you in some way, often through the Scriptures. He did this for me long after I started writing this book.

RESOLVING SERIOUS DOUBTS

One particular night, as I lay in bed, I experienced some serious doubts and misgivings. Had I really heard from God? Or did I just think I did? I asked God and drifted off to sleep.

When I came before the Lord the next morning, immediately, even as I was sitting down at my desk, my eyes fell upon a passage of scripture in my opened Bible, and I read these words:

My heart is inditing a good matter: I speak of the things which I have made touching the king: my tongue is the pen of a ready writer.   Psalm 45:1

Wow! I was "bowled over" by that. Needless to say, that momentary experience took care of all my doubt.

Later in the writing process, there came another moment when I was being "bothered" by my inabilities with grammar, and again God, by His Holy Spirit, told me that it was not that I could but that I would. He is ready and able to help our faltering faith, especially when you ask Him.

THE JUST SHALL LIVE BY FAITH

As we noted in an earlier chapter, God's Word declares:

The just shall live by faith.   Romans 1:17

167

God not only spoke this to the early Roman Christians; He's still saying it today: *"The just shall live by faith."* Faith in whom or what? Well, faith in the living God and Father, and faith in Jesus, His beloved Son. This God kind of faith is not having faith in yourself; it's having faith in God. And there's a big difference. You may have faith in yourself or your own abilities, but you need faith in God, faith that He exists and faith that He will do what He has promised to do. When you believe this, He is with you in the doing of it. How "cool" is that?

God is a wonderful Helper, and we were never meant to live a life apart from Him. Instead, we are meant to live with Him and by Him every single day. It isn't enough just to have fellowship and communion with God on Sunday morning. He is our heavenly Father, His Son, Jesus Christ, is our personal Savior, and His Holy Spirit is our constant Comforter and Guide.

HERE'S THE QUESTION

But here's the question: What did we know at some point that we allowed time and distractions to rob us of? What did we have at some point that we allowed to slip away from us? What did we believe that we no longer believe? What mattered a lot to us, and it no longer does? Take time to think about this.

You can do this now, or you can do it over a period of days. Let these questions simmer in your spirit and in your thoughts. Why? So that you can rekindle what you once had. The fire of your faith may have gone out, or it may be nearly out. Let the breath of God blow on it for a while, and let it be rekindled. In prayer, let your faith be stirred up, so that it flames into life again. Then, get serious about tending to what you believed for in the first place, thus giving faith a chance.

WHY DO SOME THINGS TAKE SO LONG?

I don't know why some things seem to take so long with God, but one thing is for sure: You must not be quick to become weary or to say, "times up," or "it should be happening by now," so that you quit or slowly cease. No, dear reader, you need to resist these thoughts and actions and stay steady. Stay in faith because whenever God has promised something, then it will surely come to pass. So, just make sure you know your part and are doing your part, and then trust God for the rest. Stay in your faith and, yes, speak out loud the very word He gave you.

I must add something else here, and that is: unbelief and unbelieving words are "big-time" faith stoppers. If you want to stop, or hinder, the move or work of God, just don't believe Him, and then you're sure to miss out on what He wanted to do. It is sad to say that even Jesus could do little when He was confronted with the people's unbelief. I know I have touched on this already, but you really need to get this truth.

HOLD STEADY

I often think of Sarah, the wife of Abraham. She got

way ahead of God and was out of faith and into self. She actually laughed at God's promise to Abraham. Then, when it seemed that God was taking way too long to fulfill what He had promised this couple (a child), Sarah, with Abraham's consent, decided to take matters into her own hands. Does that sound familiar? Most women tend to "jump the gun," so to speak, and force things to happen before their time. Because of this, they complicate their life without purposing to do so.

I, at times, have to say to myself, "Hold steady and stay in faith. Don't get ahead of yourself, even though others may be saying this or that." Yes, doubt comes and wondering and wavering too, but now I know something new that I didn't know before, and it's that we must give faith a chance.

What does this mean? It means give God time to do things on His own schedule and in His own way. Everything has its time and season, and, besides, it's never wise to hasten something that is not quite ready or mature.

ELIJAH HEARD "A SOUND OF ABUNDANCE OF RAIN"

I love the story of Elijah sending his servant to see if any rain seemed imminent (see 1 Kings 18:41-45). He was praying for rain, and rightly so, for it had not rained for so long that the land was in a three-year famine.

Elijah would pray and then he would send the servant to look toward the sea to see if any rain seemed to be coming. He had done this six times already, but each time the servant returned to say that he saw nothing. The seventh time was to be different.

This time, the servant returned to say that he saw a very small cloud, Elijah responded that the servant should prepare a chariot and rush to tell King Ahab the news, lest the coming rain deter him. Before anything at all was visible, in the Spirit, Elijah had heard *"a sound of abundance of rain"* (verse 41). Sure enough, the much needed rain came.

WHY SEVEN TIMES?

But why did the prophet have to pray seven times? It surely didn't mean that God wasn't hearing him. It meant that Elijah was calling forth something in the land. It was something that God wanted to happen and had placed in the heart of the prophet, but Elijah had to use his mouth to call it into existence.

> *I, at times, have to say to myself, "Hold steady and stay in faith. Don't get ahead of yourself!"*

When Elijah's servant saw that small cloud, the prophet knew that he could stop praying and begin rejoicing. God had heard and was answering his prayer. I really like this true story because it teaches and encourages me to keep pressing in and pressing on. When God gives you a word, hang onto it and go with it until you see it come to pass.

A good habit is to speak God's words out loud. Why should we do this? Because His angels, who do His commandments, are listening, ready to hearken to the voice of His Word (see Psalm 103:20). Speak it and see what happens.

FAITH AND FEAR, TWO PASSENGERS

Think about this. Faith and fear are like two passengers, each needing a ride. And guess what? You are the vehicle. Fear will hop onto you whenever and however it can, while faith is gentle and waits for your invitation or response.

Both of these passengers have a destination to get to, and they both need you to get them there. Once aboard, they will work to encourage you to either speak faith-based words or fear-based words.

Fear wants your words to be full of fear, and wants you to speak destructive, negative and even complaining and murmuring words, but faith only wants to speak what God, our heavenly Father, and His Word have to say.

How about giving some thought to what and who you want to take in and let ride with you. Surely your journey should have the better outcome, and it can have—if you'll just give faith a chance.

THE NEED FOR HOLY SPIRIT EMPOWERMENT

There is something else that is needful to continued faith, and I'm talking about the work and function of the Holy Spirit in your life. He is necessary to you, as He is the One who will enable you walk in the Spirit and to be sure-footed while doing it.

The Holy Spirit is spoken of "all over the place" in the Bible, from Genesis through Revelation. He is the sent One whom Jesus spoke of, when He said:

But the Comforter, which is the Holy Ghost, whom the Father will send in my name, he shall teach you all things, and bring all things to your remembrance, whatsoever I have said unto you.　　　John 14:26

We were not meant to be left alone or left to our own resources. The Father has sent us the Comforter, and He is prepared to do His work in us. If we are to maintain our faith alive and to share it with others, we must be empowered to do so.

God never intended for us to function only out of our own strength or wisdom. Therefore, I encourage you to believe for and receive the Holy Spirit and the specific gifts He has designed for you. These are not necessarily for your own good, but for helping others.

EVEN JESUS NEEDED HOLY SPIRIT EMPOWERMENT

Even Jesus, on earth as a man, needed the Holy Spirit to overshadow Him. And just as the Holy Spirit came upon Him, so we, too, need the Holy Spirit to come upon us, fill us and flow out through us.

So, dear reader, do learn more about the Holy Spirit and His work, please read the entirety of the first two chapters of the book of Acts. In this book, it isn't possible to go into great detail. But I must say that the Holy Spirit and His power are an absolute necessity in our journey of life, and without Him we cannot be empowered to do the works of Christ.

Each of us would be lost without the Spirit's leading in our lives. He is present when we are born again and also when we are baptized in water, but this is just the beginning of our experiences with Him. There is much more, as the disciples of Jesus learned.

> *The same Holy Ghost is present in the world today to enable those who open their hearts to Him!*

THE DISCIPLES, TOO, NEEDED HOLY GHOST EMPOWERMENT

Just before Jesus was taken back up to Heaven, He gave a series of commandments to His disciples. They included these words:

Go ye therefore, and teach all nations, baptizing them in the name of the Father, and of the Son, and of the

Holy Ghost: teaching them to observe all things what-
soever I have commanded you: and, lo, I am with you
alway, even unto the end of the world. Amen.

Matthew 28:19-20

But how could humble and mostly uneducated men carry out a program so vast and demanding? The answer, of course, was that they couldn't—in themselves. That's why Jesus promised them that they would soon be empowered by the Holy Spirit:

For John truly baptized with water; but ye shall be
baptized with the Holy Ghost not many days hence.

Acts 1:5

But ye shall receive power, after that the Holy Ghost is
come upon you: and ye shall be witnesses unto me
both in Jerusalem, and in all of Judaea, and in
Samaria, and unto the uttermost part of the earth.

Acts 1:8

THE FULFILLMENT OF THE PROMISE

How interesting that the fulfillment of these promises came on what was known as the day of Pentecost, a Jewish feast day, fifty days later:

And when the day of Pentecost was fully come, they
were all with one accord in one place. And suddenly
there came a sound from heaven as of a rushing mighty

wind, and it filled all the house where they were sit-ting. And there appeared unto them cloven tongues like as of fire, and it sat upon each of them. And they were all filled with the Holy Ghost, and began to speak with other tongues, as the Spirit gave them utterance.

Acts 2:1-4

So why am I telling you about an amazing event that occurred so many years ago? Because the same Holy Ghost is present in the world today to enable those who open their hearts to Him. With His help, we, too, can become witnesses, just like the early disciples, for the Lord desires that the process of the spreading of His Word and the building of His Kingdom in the hearts of men to continue.

JUST RIGHT FOR EACH OF US

We must give our faith a chance to grow and go on to maturity so that we can each serve God in the unique way He has prepared for us. Whatever that is, know that it will be just right for you. He has known your purpose from the beginning of time and He will empower you to fulfill it. So give your faith a chance to believe and receive from God.

If you have questions, that's okay. Ask away, and you'll receive the witness of the Holy Spirit to your spirit. Just don't sit back in doubt or, worse yet, unbelief, for you can know the truth for sure.

In the case that you don't receive all the answers you

would like, know that what God gives will be exactly what you need. He doesn't give us everything at once because we couldn't handle it. He feeds you little by little, so don't debate Him on His ways or His Word. Just go on with God.

GOD'S LEADING

I asked God to lead me even as I was writing this to you. His way is always to lead us with and to the truth, and what He does is always based on His good Word.

Your faith was not meant to be parked somewhere, waiting for the return of Christ or you waiting to be taken out in the Rapture of the Church. Oh no! Dear reader, your faith was meant to journey with the heavenly Father, and you can do this through the promise and gift of the Holy Ghost. With His help, you will give faith a chance and cause it to go on and on. ❧

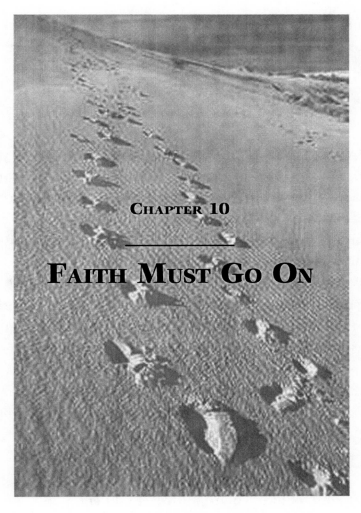

CHAPTER 10

FAITH MUST GO ON

*And the things that thou hast heard of me among many
witnesses, the same commit thou to faithful men, who
shall be able to teach others also.* 2 Timothy 2:2

Faith must go on. Why? Because it was not meant to
be contained, hidden or kept to yourself. That's the
world's way of trying to keep you and God separate. It's

rather like being put in a corner and told to stay there in your place. The world wants to contain your faith, but God wants it to break free of every restraint.

The Loosing of Opposing Things

At the same time the world wants to contain your faith, it has loosed all sorts of opposing things all around us. While all that is good and right is being shoved aside, all that is evil is now given free reign. As we've all heard, if you hear a lie repeated enough times, after a while it somehow becomes truth to you.

We are wonderfully free here in these United States, but there are some freedoms that are not totally beneficial. Do give heed to what God said through St. Paul to the Corinthians, something we all still need to hear:

All things are lawful unto me, but all things are not expedient: all things are lawful for me, but I will not be brought under the power of any.

1 Corinthians 6:12

It sounds like we are all free to do good, and we are also free to do evil. And some do so, without restraint. When choosing what freedoms we should experience, we need to ask the question: will this be good for my body, my soul and my spirit? Also, will this be good for me spiritually, even emotionally? Why? For even bondage may only look entertaining and/or be enjoyable at first, so it will be welcomed without much thought. But do know, child, that it can have a "kick" that you may not have bargained for (see 1 Corinthians 6:12 and 10:23). So do beware of the hidden consequences. Of course, evil is not always seen as what it really is, and those who try to warn others are denounced and made sport of.

Notice the word *power*? You might want to consider it. I know I did one day with this thought: "could I be brought under the power of any? Have I been brought under the power of any?" I thought about it enough to cause me to pray to God that I not be brought under the power of any.

Every time the Holy Spirit brings this verse to my mind, I immediately pray that word. Why do this immediate kind of praying? Because God knows what's ahead, and we don't, and those quick, seconds-long prayers are for your immediate benefit and welfare. I know this isn't totally related to faith going on, but it's a little about faith being hindered and, worse yet, being stopped from going on.

Faith in God means believing in Him, in what He's about, in what He says and in what He does ... in what He wants to be done!

181

Directing Your Faith

There are many types of faith. As I noted previously, there is faith in yourself, in your talents and abilities. There is also faith in what you can't do—a negative faith. There is also faith in the world and what it has to offer.

Most people don't look beyond those obvious focuses, but what about faith in God Himself? Faith in Him means believing in Him, in what He's about, in what He says and in what He does. True faith in God goes beyond even this. It believes in His will, what He wants to come forth or to be done in any given situation.

Most of us have been taught to pretty much depend upon ourselves, but what happens when you run out of knowledge or ability? Don't you sometimes empty out? I have experienced this in the past, and I still do occasionally. And, really, this is okay, although it's not comfortable or pleasurable, and is sometimes frustrating. Still, the important thing is to know what to do when it happens.

When I run out of gas, so to speak, I see myself as a needle and my life as a thread, and I see that God has the whole spool. So, when I run out, I just go to Him for more. He is and He has more than enough. There are no shortages with this great and almighty God. He is called the Most High for a reason (for example, see Psalm 9:2).

Giving Out Requires that We Be Replenished

Perhaps you have given and given until you're "running on empty" yourself. That's no problem. Our great

God, by Christ Jesus, can very easily fill you up again. He'll not only fill your cup; He'll cause it to run over.

David of old learned this secret (see Psalm 23). Check that wonderful psalm out, and while you're there, stop long enough to get your cup refilled.

Could it be that you are really in need of strengthening? If so, do what the Bible speaks of in Isaiah:

> But they that wait upon the LORD shall renew their strength; they shall mount up with wings as eagles; they shall run, and not be weary; and they shall walk, and not faint. Isaiah 40:31

If you are faithful to wait upon the Lord, your faith will then continue on. So staying in the Lord's presence until your strength is renewed is surely worth whatever wait is required. I have often taken God at His Word and sat patiently in a chair, reminding Him of what He had said about renewing our strength if we wait upon Him. And, sure enough, He did exactly what He had promised. I can't explain how He does it, because it's a God work and surely beyond my comprehension, but I can say with certainty that He does it.

And, yes, there are other resources we can call on to be strengthened, but when God does it, He strengthens all of you—body, soul and spirit.

Faith Is Your Vehicle

Please never discount your faith. It's your vehicle to

move you along on this journey. It enables you to go on with God, with yourself and with others.

God believes in you and me and wants us to move on and out with our faith. He never leaves us alone in this walk. He's always with us in our faith.

Plus, He tells us to *"prove all things"* and *"try the spirits"*:

> **Go ahead. Ask Him. "What is Your word on this or that?"**

Prove all things; hold fast that which is good.

1 Thessalonians 5:21

Beloved, believe not every spirit, but try the spirits whether they are of God: because many false prophets are gone out into the world.

1 John 4:1

So go ahead. Ask Him. "What is Your word on this or that?"

Do I do this all the time? No, I'm still learning, but I do it when I'm not sure about what action to take or not to take. Always remember that God knows. I'm aware of the fact that I've said this before, but it's brought such comfort and help to me throughout the years that I want it for you too. This is what keeps my faith steady while I'm in the process of sorting through anything I encounter in the way.

Dear reader, your faith was meant to grow, never to stagnate. When you think about it, everything that's alive grows and produces. Your life with God and with Christ Jesus is a living, breathing relationship. It was never meant to be a religion or to become stagnated in religious tradition. So do let that relationship come into being, and then let it thrive and grow.

WHAT CHURCH TO ATTEND?

It's important to find a church that recognizes the Trinity: the Father, the Son and the Holy Ghost. It's also important to find a church that uses the Bible, God's written Word, as its source of wisdom, direction, guidance, counsel and more. It's foolish for anyone to try to rely on human intelligence alone. As we noted earlier, God has said:

Come now, and let us reason together.   Isaiah 1:18

Years ago, when I asked a church leader why he wasn't seeking God for the wisdom he needed for some matters before him, he answered me, "I don't need to. God gave me a brain and intelligence, and I'm going to use it." Well, of course, he was right in the fact that God gave us intelligence, but He never intended for us to use it apart from Him.

He has said very plainly in His Word:

Trust in the LORD with all thine heart; and lean not on unto thine own understanding. In all thy ways acknowledge him, and he shall direct thy paths.
                                        Proverbs 3:5-6

So stay connected to God to get His direction for you.

GOD WITH US

God meant for our faith to endure, and for it to endure, it must be faith in Him first. When we have faith in Him, then He is *"with"* us, and we are blessed.

When you read the Bible, you will find it peppered with this phrase, that God was *"with"* a specific person. For example, consider Joseph in captivity in Egypt:

> *And his master [Potiphar] saw that the LORD was with him, and that the LORD made all that he did to prosper in his hand.* Genesis 39:3

> *The keeper of the prison looked not to any thing that was under his hand; because the LORD was with him, and that which he did, the LORD made it to prosper.* Genesis 39:23

Men and women who were blessed and succeeded in Bible days found that grace because God was *"with"* them. I don't know about you, but I surely need Him to be *"with"* me too. Our world may be very different from the ancient world of Bible days, but we still need God's presence *"with"* us today.

TAKING A STAND

There is a desperate need in our generation for men

and women who will stand up for what they believe and for what has been passed down to us, all the way from Genesis to the end of Revelation. We need those who will get into a relationship with God and then stay in that relationship.

We can all be sure that there will be temptations coming our way, but we can also know that we can resist the devil, and he will flee from us. This is God's promise:

Submit yourselves therefore to God. Resist the devil, and he will flee from you.   James 4:7

Will he always go quickly? Not necessarily, but he certainly doesn't like to be reminded of what God has said. Therefore you need to repeat those promises out loud and keep repeating them out loud until he leaves you alone. Rather than give in to his will, let praises to God spring up within you. Rejoice in the Lord, and when the trial has ended, you can seal it with a great shout of victory.

STANDING ALONE?

Faith must go on even though, at times, it will seem like you are standing alone in your faith. When this happens, don't worry about it, and don't stop believing. Just stand, and you will prevail.

There are constant battles in the spirit world for your faith. If you don't think so, get your head out of the sand. The God you believe in is being mocked, cursed and made fun of. Many dispersions are being cast upon His Word.

Still, many of God's people remain silent (I'm just as guilty). Some religions would rise up and issue death threats if you did that to their god.

It's not that our God needs defending, for He's a mighty God to be sure, but to be silent, while He's being defied and defamed and while those who are against Him and His Christ get stronger every day, also cannot be right. Let us learn to stand for what we believe.

THE FIRES OF PERSECUTION

The battles being waged against marriage and against your children are like forest fires, quickly sweeping through and destroying much good land. This is a big and strong spiritual battle against God and His people, and that includes you. In reality, it's nothing new; it's been going on for thousands of years. Just make sure you withstand it and stay on your feet, spiritually speaking.

Faith must go on, and it will go on because the Scriptures promise:

Upon this rock I will build my church; and the gates of hell shall not prevail against it.　　Matthew 16:18

The true Church, the Body of Christ, is made up of all believers everywhere, and therefore it is alive and well and going forward in the power and wisdom of God. But not everyone stays onboard. If you become lukewarm in your faith, God has said that He will spit you out of His mouth:

So then because thou art luke-warm, and neither cold nor hot, I will spue thee out of my mouth.
Revelation 3:16

It's time for your faith to be white hot, time to stir up the gifts of God within you and to be and do what God has given you faith for in the first place. It's time for you to respond to His ways and His plan of growth for you.

First, He wants you to get with and in Him. Then He wants you to be strengthened and to receive grace and mercy in your time of need. Then, you need to find out what His battle plan is for you, for your family and for your country.

FEAR TACTICS

There is a battle going on against you, and the most important tactic being used is fear. Fear is a spirit. If that were not true, why would God have said it?

For God hath not given us the spirit of fear; but of power, and of love, and of a sound mind.   2 Timothy 1:7

There is a desperate need in our generation for men and women who will stand up for what they believe and for what has been passed down to us!

189

Like it or not, believe it or not, there is indeed a spiritual battle going on, and you and yours are the targets. Stand in faith against fear, and drive it out.

FAITH IN GOD IS VITAL

Can you see now why your faith in God in so vital? Faith and fear don't mix, so don't try to make them coexist. When you begin to compromise with the world, your faith will slowly erode. It's always best to kick fear out at its onset, while it's much easier to get rid of.

God has a word for every situation you will face in life. Just seek Him and ask Him for that specific word. Ask Him for His thoughts on any subject. Usually you won't have to wait long for His answer.

If you do have to wait at times, so what? What God gives you is always worth waiting for, and what He reveals to you will not be anything you could have thought of on your own.

WHEN WE SEEM NOT TO GET AN ANSWER

But what about the times when it seems that we get no answer at all to our requests? Well, one thing we know. It's not that God is not hearing us. So, His silence could mean "no," and His *no*s are okay. When you don't like God's *no*s (and who hasn't experienced them?), ask Him to help you come into agreement with His will. If you can do that, you'll be a lot happier in life. Wouldn't you like for your child, especially your teenagers, to take that attitude with you? That could make for a lot more peace and harmony within the family.

Not always having our own way or getting all that we want is, at times, a blessing in disguise. Our struggles with the will of God may be what's making our faith grow. That fact, too, may be disguised. I like what Saint Peter wrote to the Church:

Simon Peter, a servant and an apostle of Jesus Christ, to them that have obtained like precious faith with us through the righteousness of God and our Saviour Jesus Christ: grace and peace be multiplied unto you through the knowledge of God, and of Jesus our Lord, according as his divine power hath given unto us all things that pertain unto life and godliness, through the knowledge of him that hath called us to glory and virtue: whereby are given unto us exceeding great and precious promises: that by these ye might be partakers of the divine nature, having escaped the corruption that is in the world through lust.

And beside this, giving all diligence, add to your faith virtue; and to virtue knowledge; and to knowledge temperance; and to temperance patience; and to patience godliness; and to godliness brotherly kindness; and to brotherly kindness charity. For if these things be in you, and abound, they make you that ye shall neither be barren nor unfruitful in the knowledge of our Lord Jesus Christ.

But he that lacketh these things is blind, and cannot see afar off, and hath forgotten that he was purged

> **What God gives you is always worth waiting for, and what He reveals to you will not be anything you could have thought of on your own!**

from his old sins. Wherefore the rather, brethren, give diligence to make your calling and election sure: for if ye do these things, ye shall never fall: for so an entrance shall be ministered unto you abundantly into the everlasting kingdom of our Lord and Saviour Jesus Christ. 2 Peter 1:1-11

This is what happens when faith goes on. It sounds like a lot, and I suppose it is. But it's all good. It certainly sounds like we will have a grand entrance coming into the everlasting Kingdom of our Lord and Savior, Jesus Christ.

CHECK YOUR WORDS

In the meantime, I would encourage you to check what you're saying. Are your words faith-filled or fear-filled?

What are you listening to? If you're listening to the popular media and picking up what is said there, then you'll have fear-filled words. If you're listening to God and picking up, by His Spirit, what

He's saying, you'll have faith-filled words. Of course, what you turn to is your choice, although we cannot say that for many countries today, since the Gospel of Christ is not allowed to be presented there, nor is the Bible allowed to be brought in. And those that do use God's Word in those nations are putting themselves at great risk, to say the very least.

What you believe and what you say is your choice, but you must know it's importance. Much of what you believe and speak will come to pass. For example, some say, "I always get a cold in February," and sure enough, they do. As we noted in an earlier chapter, God has declared this:

Death and life are in the power of the tongue.
                                                Proverbs 18:21

So listen to what you're saying. Listen also to what is being said to you, and stop agreeing with those idle but destructive words. Remember that Jesus was able to stop a storm with His words (see Mark 4:39). Your fear-filled words can bring a forecast storm to reality. Instead, pray it away. You have a choice. To whom will you yield your tongue?

I know that being careful about our words is easier said than done, and I'm still learning this lesson. Ask God to help you set a watch upon your mouth and to keep the door of your lips (see Psalm 141:3). I do this, especially when God, by His Spirit, brings this particular verse to

193

my mind. When this happens, I immediately pray these powerful words.

It's Just Talk

At first, it's not easy to control the tongue. Some don't even see the need to do it. "It's just talk," they say. But some of it is careless talk, and some of our words, spoken in jest, can deeply hurt others. They're just words, but they can be like arrows, piercing right into the heart and leaving deep wounds that sometimes last a lifetime.

What you speak matters, even when speaking to your children. Calling your child names or saying unkind words about them in a moment of anger or frustration does great damage, especially if it happens repeatedly. In a child's mind, it's impossible to sort things out and know when you didn't really mean what you were saying and when you did. A child comes to believe what is said about them or to them and often comes to feel less confident because of it. And that's just the opposite of what should be happening.

Could it be that faith and words go hand in hand? God believed, and He spoke, and all that He said came to pass. Are we not like our Creator in this regard? Whether we want to accept it or not, this is the case. We also believe and we also speak, but is our belief lined up with His belief, and are our words lined us with His words? They can be, for sure, little by little. It's just do you want to be made in His image and likeness?

MADE IN GOD'S IMAGE

I don't know about you, but this is my desire. My image hasn't been so great, not even good. Actually it has been poor. But with and by God's good Word and His grace and love, it has been slowly changing. This is not always visible to everyone around me, for I am still in the remodelling stage. But one day, as He continues on with His work in me, this cup will be ready for service.

How about you? Are you ready for change, a God change, one that can truly transform? He is good at it, and He always has the best in mind for you.

DON'T LET ANYTHING PREVENT YOU

Your faith in God is important, and so you want it to go on. Don't let anything keep this from happening. If you've gotten derailed, put off by circumstances or by people's words or deeds, get up and go on.

Forgive them, and if you think you can't do it, or you're having a hard time doing it, ask God to help you. He will. How do I know? One day, while I was at my dining room table, I sensed God wanting me to forgive a certain person. I said to Him, "I can't. I just can't. They did this thing on purpose."

So there I was in this unasked-for moment with God. I sensed that He was waiting for a very different response from me and that I didn't have long to give it.

I was caught in a dilemma. I wanted to do what God was saying, but I really could not. I just couldn't get past my own feelings. The only thing I knew to do in that moment was to say to God, "Please help me!" I no sooner said it than there was a sudden gush of great compassion rising up within me, and I found myself saying, "Oh God, I do forgive! I do! And I'm so sorry for not wanting to do it in the first place!" The Lord had marvelously answered my cry.

WHY AM I TELLING YOU THIS?

Why am I telling you this? Perhaps it's so that you can see there's a way for you to forgive, as there was for me. Not forgiving those who have wronged us is sometimes like having a ball and chain attached to us. It binds both us and them. God wants His people to be set free and healed, and often that requires forgiveness on our part.

Faith must go on, that God kind of faith, and your failure to forgive others can hinder you much more than you realize. God is love, and He loves you. I know that I've been saying that a lot in this book, but it's because it's so important. God has a life for you and a journey of faith for you to go on, and you will not do it alone, but with Him.

GET UP!

God has a lot to say to you from His Word, the Bible, so get up and spend time with Him. Ask Him, "What would You like to talk about?" and then allow Him to direct you, so that you can hear and understand and come to know Him better.

One day, on that great and terrible Day of Judgment, you'll be so glad you did this. On that day, Jesus will speak on your behalf before the Father, and entrance into His Kingdom will be granted to you. What a wonderful day that will be! You must make sure you get there, so make sure your faith goes on.   ✿

CHAPTER 11

WHY BLAME GOD?

And I heard a loud voice saying in heaven, Now is come salvation, and strength, and the kingdom of our God, and the power of his Christ: for the accuser of our brethren is cast down, which accused them before our God day and night. And they overcame him by the blood of the Lamb, and by the word of their testimony; and they loved not their lives unto the death. Revelation 12:10-11

> *I want to ask you very directly: what have you been saying in your heart, or maybe nursing over for weeks, months or even years without verbalizing?*

Blame God? Why not? Martha did! In the biblical account of the death of Lazarus, which also tells of his two sisters, Mary and Martha, Martha blamed the Lord for not having been there:

Lord, if thou hadst been here, my brother had not died.

John 11:21

Was she right to blame Him?

WHO'S TO BLAME?

And how about you? I want to ask you very directly: what have you been saying in your heart, or maybe nursing over for weeks, months or even years without verbalizing? Are you like Martha? Do you question, wonder and then finally blame God for whatever happens in your life? After all, He's God. Why didn't He intervene? He certainly could have, and it probably seems to you that He should have.

Many of us have thought or said, "Why is this happening? Why wasn't that stopped before it could happen? Why wasn't it prevented from happening in the first place?" It's easy to blame God, but could the blame be elsewhere? What if our thoughts have been dead-end thoughts, going no-where? Could it be that our thoughts are in need of correction? Do we need a different direction in life, and we haven't yet realized it?

Can we really blame God for anything? Think about that. It doesn't make good sense, but we do it anyway. Again, it's easy to do, and it's a lot harder to dig in and find out what is really going on—probably within our-selves.

I don't know if we can ever get all the answers, but surely we can get enough of them to satisfy ourselves and then to move on. For me, asking God to speak to me through His Word makes all the difference in the world. His Word has settled many issues for me and put to rest many doubts, much confusion and many worries that I had.

A POEM AND A PRAYER

I want to include here a poem, a prayer, that I wrote one morning after crying out to God for His help and ask-ing Him to speak to me through His Word. I was very overwhelmed with the circumstances of my life, and I really needed Him. He inspired me with these words. They came to me after I meditated on three scripture passages: Psalm 43:3, Isaiah 55:7-8 and Philippians 2:5. I trust that it will speak to you as well.

LEAD ME, LORD JESUS

Lead me, Lord Jesus. Lead me, Lord Jesus.
Send out Your light and Your truth.
Lead me, Lord Jesus. Lead me, Lord Jesus
Away from unrighteous thoughts.
Forsaking them all, forsaking them all,
Now on to Your higher ways and thoughts.
Lead me, Lord Jesus. Lead me, Lord Jesus
To thoughts of good, not worry or fear,
Not on the lacks or the problems so near.
Lead me, Lord Jesus. Lead me, Lord Jesus.
Lead me, Lord Jesus, my Friend.
I let the mind of Christ be in me.
I let the mind of Christ be in me.
For that's what I hear, that's what I hear.
That's what I hold ever so dear.
Lead me, Lord Jesus. Lead me, Lord Jesus.

My problems didn't go away, but I found a way to work through them, and that was by looking to the dear Lord Jesus. So the poem has become an ongoing prayer for me.

OUR DEAR LORD

I use the word *dear* for the Lord Jesus because He has become very dear to me, as is His sent Helper, Comforter and Teacher, the Holy Spirit. So really, do you still want to blame God for your problems? Can one who is all love and who commands us to love be blamed for anything bad?

It's a good thing our God is so longsuffering, patient, slow to anger, slow to speak and quick to hear and that He has new mercies waiting for us every morning. He has great compassion for us in our daily situations and wants more for us than we can ever know.

So, do you want to bite the very hand that feeds you, when there is a throne of grace to go to instead? As noted earlier, we go there to get mercy and find grace to help in time of need (see Hebrews 4:16). God has a way to help you out of every difficulty, and so blaming Him will get you nowhere.

The help God offers us comes through Jesus, who is the Word of God, and through the Holy Spirit. He extends to us His wonderful grace and mercy and many other things that we don't yet understand and haven't yet been able to receive.

THROUGH JESUS CHRIST, OUR LORD

Many years ago, Bob and I belonged to a group at our Catholic church that met to compose the prayers that were to be said during the Sunday Mass. On one occasion, as we were reading through the material we had been given, I noticed something. Spread throughout the prayers were the words *"through Jesus Christ."* It seemed that nearly every phrase ended with that, and this got me to wondering. Why was that? Why was everything *through Jesus Christ*?

As the others were talking, I was going over and over this in my mind. Why? Why is this? Then, suddenly, I knew. I really knew! God, by His Spirit, had revealed it to me.

Everything had to be *through Jesus Christ* because He is the Door by which we enter into the Kingdom of God. There is no other way. Jesus Christ Himself is *"the way, the truth, and the life"* (John 14:6).

And Jesus is to be worshiped. As we noted early on, I knew that the angels worshipped Him (see Hebrews 1:6). And since angels worship Him, how could I do any less? By the way, everything in the spiritual realm knows this about Jesus being the only way, truth and life. Is it any wonder that the enemies of Christ would have you and me kept in the dark and tempted with doubts and unbelief? How could one who has been dead for more than two thousand years still command attention and interest and speculation? Believe me, there is one person and one person alone before whom all will have to stand and give an accounting, and it's not Saint Peter, but Jesus Christ Himself.

THE GOD MOMENTS IN MY LIFE

I think of these God-moments in my life as stop-and-make-a-new-start places. Maybe we could call them life's little intersections. Much like a vehicle approaching a stop sign is required by law to come to a complete stop, we experience a lot of stops in life too. And God has a plan for all of them.

A vehicle that approaches a stop sign, of course, doesn't stay stopped. It just pauses there a moment to make sure the way is clear, and then it goes on. Could it be that the stops in our life are really just pauses we need to take, and we're not meant to be so quick to move on to what we want or what we have planned? Could it be that God, our heavenly Father, has other and better ideas and plans for us?

Who knows? Maybe this book has been written just for you. And maybe God wants you to know that you need to stop and think about where you are in your life, where you're going, what you're doing and where He is involved in it all. He does want to walk and talk with you every day. So, rather then continuing on your merry way, do pause and consider God and your relationship with Him. He has a journey for you. He wants you to stop and think about this. Why? Because it's time for your journey with Him to soon begin.

Maybe this book has been written just for you!

Please know, it's not an obligation to have, but rather a relationship to have, now and forever. It will be a little like a garden, as both your physical life and your spiritual life need to be tended to, cared for, watered and nourished. This may sound like a lot of work, and at times it is, but it's worth it all!

It's Worth It All

If you don't tend to your spiritual garden, who will? You need God's Son. You need His Word. It's life for you. It's like a seed that can be planted in you and will eventually bear fruit and produce a great harvest. So you don't want to miss what God has for you. He has prepared for you a unique life experience that can be full and amazing.

You will be amazed when you see Him moving in your life. He moves in big things and also in small things, and He moves in the ordinary and in the extraordinary.

God Will Move for You

For example, God will provide you a parking space up close to where you're going. He will give you favor with a clerk who doesn't want to give you a refund because the designated time to return your merchandise has expired. Those were little things He did for me.

Then there were the "biggies." For example, my toddler awoke in the middle of the night with an earache, when we were away camping in the middle of no-where-ville. I cried out to God, saying, "A nurse I'm not. I don't know what to do. Please help my child," and somehow and some way, He did it.

These are examples that immediately come to my mind, and I suppose if you thought about it, God has been there for you in many ways already too—even if you didn't realize it at the time.

NEITHER GIVE PLACE TO THE DEVIL

Recently God spoke to me through the words of Saint Paul's letter to the Ephesians: *"Neither give place to the devil"* (Ephesians 4:27). I had read that verse many times, but somehow I had never given it the thought it deserved. I now made a note to make sure I prayed this for myself and my family. It's not that we intend to give place to the devil in our lives. We don't. But sometimes we do it unwittingly.

When I think of this phrase "giving place to the devil," I think of it as making room for him in some way. Maybe we make room for, or allow into our lives, things that should not be given entrance. They may seem harmless at the time, but, without knowing it or wanting it, we have opened a door through which the devil can come right in.

Fighting among ourselves and allowing the expression of explosive anger can do that, and failing to resolve anger issues quickly is even more deadly. As we noted earlier, God said it this way in context:

Be ye angry, and sin not: let not the sun go down upon your wrath: neither give place to the devil.
Ephesians 4:26-27

When Satan comes in in this way and does us harm, who then gets the blame? Only rarely do we recognize that we have opened a door to him ourselves.

CUTTING OFF YOUR FAITH

Have you thought that blaming God for everything may be cutting off your faith. How could this be? Well, when we direct blame at God, it's a little like chopping at the very bridge that can enable you to cross over to the other side. I know it's hard not to, when life gets difficult, but know, dear reader, that's when you need your faith and belief in God.

If your prayers have not been answered, why not ask God the reason behind it!

So, what will you do with your measure of faith? Will you cast it aside because someone hurt or offended you or maybe spoke wrongly to you, when they should have known better? Have you, without knowing, undermined your own faith by praying sincerely to God and putting your faith in Him and then later speaking just the opposite of His will and promise with your own tongue? Do you then blame God for not answering or not hearing your prayers?

If your prayers have not been answered, why not ask God the reason behind it. Can He err? Never! Maybe, instead, have you put your faith on a shelf? "How's that?" you may ask. By saying to yourself, "I'll do it later when I have more time." The problem is that we never know how much time we have. Life on earth, even for those who live longest, is short. Eternity, however, is forever, and where will you spend it? If this is not an important issue with you, it had better become one.

Many have become wholly consumed by this world and its pleasures, thinking that this is all there is to life. Well, I have some good news for you. There's a whole lot more ahead of us. Some of us will receive rewards and even crowns. If you have become convinced that you will come back here in some other form, then think again. Kick that lie out the door and begin to think on the truths that are so important and necessary for you to hear. And the following is one example:

A Rich Man's Lament

A certain rich man, when he had died, suddenly found himself in a place he surely didn't like or want to be, but it was too late for him to do anything about it. The moment he opened his eyes, he was in Hell and in torment.

Somehow this man was able to see Abraham afar off, and he begged him to send someone to his father's house and testify to his five brothers, so they would not come to the same place of torment. Father Abraham answered him in this way:

They have Moses and the prophets; let them hear them.

Luke 16:29

I won't take time and space here to tell the whole story. What is important is that there is a forever place that you want to avoid at all costs, and to do that you need to give ear and heed what God is saying while you still have time. If you have not yet been willing to listen to God through the people He used to write His Word or through those He has sent to you personally (even though they might not do or say what you would prefer), please heed them now. Be alert and welcoming to those God sends to you, give ear to their message and do what you can and should with it. If you're unsure about what you have heard, seek God for understanding or counsel, even confirmation, for He will surely give it to anyone who asks.

Hold On to Faith and Hope

Hold on to faith and hope. As we noted in Chapter 3, God's Word teaches us:

And let us not be weary in welldoing: for in due season we shall reap, if we faint not.   Galatians 6:9

This word was written so many years ago, and yet it is still needful for us to hear in these days of the twenty-first century.

So take heart, dear reader, and take heed—instead of blaming someone else or complaining, which too often just turns into a venting of your anger or frustration. You really need to get past that. Fume if you must, but make it short. Release your steam, but then put your energies into seeking God for His strength, wisdom and grace. Ask Him for a solution to what ails you or besets you or whatever your need may be.

Then keep seeking God until you find what you're looking for. Ask Him for His thoughts and His way about anything or anyone. Ask Him when you don't understand His truths. He doesn't want you, or anyone else, to be kept in the dark. Ask Him to shine His light so brightly across your path that you can't miss it. He's able and willing to do that.

Then, if the answers seem slow in coming, avoid blaming God. Instead, you might want to blame the interference coming from those who are so opposed to God, His Christ, His Spirit and you, His creation.

FINALLY, KNOW THIS

Finally, please know this. This is the crux of the message of this book. Our Father in Heaven wants us to come to Him, and we do that through His Son, Jesus, the Christ, who was the sent Messiah, and we were meant to have fellowship with Him. It is through Him that we are saved, and by no other means.

So when Jesus comes to you in a quiet moment, allow Him, the Christ, who is called *"the hope of glory"* (Colossians 1:27), to come in and be with you. And so begin your journey with God, who is love. Of course, it is up to you to say yea or nay or to consider a bit longer, and if you do that, talk everything over with God.

But don't wait too long, for time may not be on your side. And if you wait too long and miss your opportunity, who will you have to blame? Will you really be able to blame God, when He is always working at bringing His creation back to its original place? That is, of us having daily fellowship with Him, plus even coming to His throne, the throne of grace.

Oh, dear reader, you really do not want to miss any of this and anything of God, the Father, His Son Jesus and the precious Holy Spirit!

THE END

Or ... is it ... the beginning?

CHAPTER 12

DEAR READER

Consider what I say; and the Lord give thee understanding in all things. 2 Timothy 2:7

Well, dear reader, I have spoken to you directly and perhaps a little too plainly, but still, I wrote from my heart and from what I know and have experienced. As you might guess, God, our heavenly Father, is still perfecting and making this little one whole in body, soul and spirit. Little by little, to be sure, and onward and upward, He leads and guides me along—even though I'm not without faults, and I stumble and lose my way. But I'm so glad not to be left to myself. He is with me every step of the way.

This book is a testimony of some of what our God has meant to me, plus some of what He has done with and for me. I've been inspired and moved by His Spirit to write about how He has worked in my life and in this, my journey, with Him that began after my new birth in Christ.

So now, dear reader, perhaps you are sensing God dealing with you. Do let this happen. You don't have to wait until you fully understand. What is important is faith and how it works. For me, I do something or function in faith and then later on, when I hear someone preach or teach the same thing or I read it, the full understanding comes. I think, "Oh, so that's what that was!" The point is that you and I don't have to know everything at first.

Here's an example for you: I know how to drive a car. Do I fully know how it all works? No. Does it matter to me? No. Why not? The mechanics of a car are just not for me to deal with, and there have been times when I have said to God (and maybe with some frustration), "A mechanic I am not." So I don't try to become one (although I'm glad for those who do have this ability), but I can seek God for the help I need and how to proceed.

You see, it's a walk-and-talk relationship with God. As I move along in this journey called life, I walk and talk with God. And He walks and talks with me along the way as well. Now, dear reader, you simply walk and talk with Him. And after a while, it will become a life of you walking, talking and doing what He has given you faith for.

You can have this too. That's one of the reasons God inspired me to write this book—for you and others, to let you know this, and the kind of life and journey to begin to have, that is especially for you.

Do fully consider this. Why? Because this is an invitation for you, dear reader, to receive Christ Jesus into your life and being, plus come to know His life for you, even to walk with the King of kings and the Lord of lords and to be a blessing.

Years ago, there was a wonderful godly teacher named Dr. Robert Cook. He was at the time President of Kings College, and he had a program on Moody Bible Radio, a station I happened upon one day when I got "fed up" with the endless commercials on other stations. (I used the radio at the time to keep me company while working in the kitchen.) Anyway, I turned the dial and kept turning it until I found a station without any commercials, and then I went no further. Without knowing it, I had stopped at a Christian station called WMBI (broadcasting from Moody Bible Institute).

One of the programs I listened to early on was with Dr. Charles Stanley and Dr. Robert Cook. Their teachings were so good, just what a hungry baby in Christ needed. Dr. Cook always ended his program with this saying: "Walk with the King, and be a blessing." Although he has been with the dear Lord a good while now, still his words stick with me, and now, many years later, I ask God at the end of my morning times with Him, to help me walk with Him and be a blessing. Am I always walking with Him and being a blessing? No, but I'm learning, little by little, to do so.

How about you? Would this be a good prayer for you too?

Would you like to hear something funny? When I do this prayer, I think of the teapot in the children's rhyme, "I'm A Little Teapot." So I also ask God to fill me up and help me pour Him out. Does that sound silly? Maybe it is, but I'm serious when I pray it.

As I finish here, let me share with you an old song that speaks to me, and maybe it will speak to you too. It's called, "In the Garden" by C. Austin Miles. I especially like the chorus. It says, "And He walks with me and He talks with me, and He tells me I am His own; and the joy we share as we tarry there, none other has ever known." Why share this with you, dear reader? Because your walk begins this way, and in your walk, you will be relating with Christ Jesus and the Spirit of God, the Holy Spirit, even our heavenly Father. And so, at first, your walk will be just like the song, where He tells you that you are His own.

And you are meant to be His own, to be sure. Believe me, it's not only the journey to begin and have, but also the daily walk and talk with Him that is important.

Really, dear reader, you do not want to miss this kind of journey with God's Son, Jesus, and His precious Holy Spirit. Think about this. Will you? Even pray and seek

God about it too. Don't wait too long, for time may not be on your side. And besides, dear reader, you surely do not want to miss the Marriage Supper of the Lamb!

Most sincerely,
Joanne Yoho
www.ajourneytobegin.com

— Notes —